Writing your Educational Research Proposal

Jodi Roffey-Barentsen

Richard Malthouse

DEDICATION

We dedicate this book to professor Mike Watts for his endless support and inspirational creative thinking.

CONTENTS

ACKNOWLEDGEMENTS

We would like to acknowledge all those students who have so generously shared their work, so that others may benefit; thank you!

INTRODUCTION

As part of the final year of your undergraduate studies you are likely to be set the task of writing a dissertation or research project. Conducting the research for this offers a great opportunity for you to investigate or explore an area of education that you are interested in.

Before you start your research, your institution or tutor will need to agree with the suitability of your project. Therefore, a research proposal usually precedes a dissertation or research project. Furthermore, in some cases, proposals are assessed as a separate module, either at Level 5 (year 2) or at Level 6 (year 3). Although most students have some idea of what they would like to investigate or explore for their research, others may find it challenging to select an appropriate topic. Choosing an area for research can be quite overwhelming – where to start? We recommend that you select a topic which holds your interest, maybe even feel passionate about. Frequently, ideas develop as a result of studying for a previous module; or sometimes they can be traced back to an experience you have had yourself, something that has affected you (or someone you know). On occasion, during these early stages of research, the selected topic(s) can be too wide or vague for the purpose of a dissertation and it is not until you start writing your proposal that you focus in on what you really want to find out. A proposal, then, offers the opportunity to plan your research in detail, as you consider the options and justify your decisions with regard to the research design. It is worth investing time into the writing of a proposal, as a detailed, well-considered proposal will make the research and writing-up of the final dissertation a much easier process. Ideally, there is a strong link between the proposal and the dissertation, as you set out what you are going to do. In reality, however, circumstances can change between the time of when the proposal was written and when the actual research takes place. In this case, the research can differ from the proposal. A proposal is, after all, a structured plan for the research, which can be amended if necessary. It may be useful to remember that research at this level, within the time available, can focus on just one very specific area; you are not trying to change the world at this stage. In the assessment of your proposal you will be judged on your approach to research, which should be systematic and with rigour; depth is more important here than the breadth or scale of your research . Most research proposals are written in third person (ie the purpose of this research is to.....), however, it is not uncommon for them to be written in first person (i.e. I would like to explore.....). We advise you check with your tutors as to which style is the preferred one.

Although different Higher Education Institutions may have their own preferred formats for a research proposal, they will almost certainly cover similar elements.

This publication contains two parts. Part one offers you advice and guidance on each of the elements of a research proposal. Part two illustrates this by offering a range of real research proposals, submitted by students on BA (Hons) in Education programmes. It must be emphasized that the proposals included, although strong ones, are largely unedited, so as not to affect their authenticity. Therefore, there may remain some inconsistencies with regard to citing and referencing or errors in spelling, grammar or syntax. We advise readers to focus on the structure of and approach to the research proposals rather than their specific content.

Part one

Elements of a Research Proposal

Typically, a research proposal contains the following elements or headings:

Pro-forma for an Educational Research Proposal

1. **Title**

2. **Introduction**

    a) Rationale

    b) Aims / purpose

    c) Research question

3. **Literature Review**

4. **Methodology / Research design**

    a) Philosophical perspective

    b) Methodology

    c) Sample / participants

    d) Methods of Data Collection

    e) Methods of Data Analysis

    f) Validity / Reliability of the study

    g) Ethical Considerations

5. References

By following these headings you will ensure that all elements of a research proposal are included and presented in a logically structured way. Next, the elements will be explained in more detail.

1. Title

As to be expected, the title of a proposal should indicate clearly what the research is about. As emphasized by Punch (2014:339): 'The title should convey as much information as possible in as few words as possible'. Part two of this book includes exemplar proposals with the following titles:

- *A case study exploring girls' perceptions of progressing to post–16 mathematics studies.*

- *An exploration into the professional development needs of Teaching Assistants supporting students with Special Educational Needs (SEN) in mainstream secondary schools.*

- *An Exploration into teachers' perceptions of the effectiveness of Learning Support Assistants, in a mainstream secondary school in Surrey.*

- *An Exploration of the Perceptions of Maths Homework for Year 10 Students.*

- *A Case Study into whether an extrinsic motivational reward will affect behaviour in a Year Five class in a South of England Primary School.*

- *Risk Taking – Good or Bad?*

Being concise and precise in your title may result in what appears to be quite dry and formal or maybe even dull. On occasion, therefore, researchers prefer a more 'catchy' title, which immediately grabs the attention of the reader. Using humour in a title, or an element of controversy or ambiguity, to provide that attention grabbing aspect, however, can be a bit of a gamble, as not everybody shares, for instance, the same sense of humour.

2. Introduction

In this part of the proposal you introduce your area for research and set the scene or contextualise the study. You need to provide a rationale for the research, stating its aims, as you explain why you think there is a 'gap' in the body of knowledge with regard to your topic. For example, Catherine sets the scene as follows, referring to relevant previous research:

> Since 2005 there has been a year on year increase in entries for AS mathematics (Department for Education (DfE, 2011, p.26). Statistics also show "high prior attaining boys are even more likely than their female counterparts to enter A level maths" (DfE, 2011, p.115). Research by Mendick (2005) and Cann (2009) state higher proportions of boys choose AS mathematics than girls.

She continues by stating the purpose of and rationale for her research:

> The purpose of this research project is to explore the factors that contribute to the lack of girls' post-16 participation in mathematics. The researcher has chosen this topic as "the mathematical skill gap"

has been highlighted as "a problem which had become acute" affecting students wishing to study Science, Technology, Engineering and Mathematics.

Dawn offers the following, listing her objectives for the study:

The aim is, defined by Walliman and Buckler (2010p63) as "the overarching purpose of the research," is to discover, explore and understand the training and professional development that Teaching Assistants feel is required to support SEN students in a mainstream secondary school effectively.

The objectives of the study are :

- *to systematically explore the issue of the training and development needs of Teaching Assistants in secondary schools by undertaking an extensive literature review*
- *to explore differing perspectives regarding the skills, knowledge and working practices that teaching assistants feel are required to effectively support secondary students with SEN and examine Teaching Assistants motivation to develop professionally, by conducting focus group/interviews in 3 mainstream secondary schools in Surrey*
- *to analyse, then synthesize the differing perspectives in an attempt to propose suggestions for professional development*

As well as 'setting the scene' and stating the rationale and aims of the research, you need to formulate a specific research question (and sub-questions, if appropriate), to present to your readers.

The examples in Part two include the following research questions:

- *What are girls' perceptions of continuing with mathematics beyond GCSE level?*

- *What are the professional development needs of teaching assistants who support students with Special Educational Needs in secondary schools?*

- *What are teachers' perceptions of the effectiveness of Learning Support Assistants in a mainstream secondary school in Surrey?*

- *In a North Hampshire secondary school, what is the Year 10 students' perspective on maths homework?*

- *Will an extrinsic motivational reward affect pupil behaviour?*

- *Are childminders provided with sufficient training and guidance to enable them to support children in taking acceptable risks? Are they reliant on personal attitudes, developed through their own experiences? Would specific training provide an alternative view?*

A 'sound' research question should have characteristics which include: being clear and unambiguous, specific, answerable with data, connected or related to each other if there is more than one question, and worthwhile asking (Punch, 2014). In other words, your research question must be answerable within the parameters of the time and resources available.

An alternative to asking a research question can be to formulate a hypothesis. A hypothesis is a statement, which the research tries to prove or disprove. The use of a hypothesis, and its associated nul-hypothesis, is more in line with the scientific or positivist paradigm and will not be discussed in this publication.

3. Literature Review

The purpose of a 'Literature Review' as part of your dissertation is to demonstrate that you are familiar with what has been written about your topic, referring to previous research, so you can relate your findings to those already published. Although you do not usually have to complete your reading at this early stage, you should identify in your proposal what literature is available. We recommended, therefore, that you start your search in the university's (on-line) library. It is usually best practice to focus on academic texts such as books and journals. The internet is also a helpful resource but you must be careful to use reliable sites only.

Gina is looking ahead and has planned a review of the following, categorizing areas into themes:

> *The Literature review will focus on key research regarding deployment and practice of Learning Support Assistants (LSAs)....The themes that have been identified are: reasons for the increase in support staff, background to recent headlines regarding the impact of LSAs; the professional status of LSAs and the effective deployment and practice of LSAs.*

Monica highlights the importance of familiarizing her with current development in her area of research:

> *The literature review will seek to find guidance through a broad spectrum of reading (Malthouse and Roffey-Barentsen, 2013) on risk taking in Early Years. The purpose of the literature review is to familiarise myself with the subject, gaining a background including others work upon the subject, and contrasting opinions (Sharp, 2009).*

4. Methodology

In this part of the proposal you explain and justify your research design. This normally starts with the philosophical assumptions or stance, also referred to as your theoretical perspective. This perspective is concerned with the way in which we understand the world and see meaning in it. The ontological question asks what is the nature of reality: "is reality of an objective nature, or the result of individual cognition?" (Cohen *et al.*, 2000:5). In other words, is reality 'out there' (objective) or is it constructed in people's minds (subjective)? The epistemological question asks how this reality can be known, or how can knowledge be acquired. In any enquiry concerned with questions of discovering knowledge and ascertaining truth, the researcher needs to be clear about their own position on how we can find out about the world; how you align yourself in this debate affects how you will go about uncovering knowledge of social behaviour (Cohen *et al.*, 2000). What you have to ask yourself is: do you see knowledge as hard, objective and tangible, or do you see it as personal and subjective, based on experience. Based on how you answer this question, you make a decision with regard to the selected paradigm. In very broad, maybe simplistic terms, there are two main paradigms to choose between: the positivist paradigm and the interpretivist paradigm.

The former is also referred to as the scientific paradigm, which requires quantitative research, whereas the latter is associated with social research, which is more aligned to qualitative research. Positivist or quantitative research seeks to measure and is scientific and objective in nature. In this type of research the researcher is separated from what is researched; in other words: an unbiased, objective outsider. The interpretivist or qualitative researcher, on the other hand, seeks to explain and is subjective. This researcher interprets the findings or data and becomes a part of the process; or: a subjective insider. So, the quantitative researcher considers reality to be real and measurable, while the qualitative researcher believes that reality is constructed by the person experiencing it. Based on these philosophical differences, you will understand that the two types of research require different research design or methodology. The positivist, scientific or quantitative researcher will usually adopt an experiment or large-scale survey as their methodology. Data collected will be in the form of numbers or statistics. Think, for instance in medicine, about testing the effectiveness of a new drug. This usually requires an experimental group, which is given the new medicine, and a control group, which is given a placebo. The control group must be very similar to the experimental group, to minimize the effects of variables other than the single independent variable (the new medicine). The effects are measured and at some point, based on these results, a decision is made on the overall effectiveness of the drug.

In social or educational research it is perhaps more appropriate to adopt an interpretivist, or qualitative methodology, as this is generally a more effective approach for explaining why something is occurring, based on people's views, perceptions or experiences. Data collected will be in the form of words or narratives. Research design or methodology here can take the form of a case study, an ethnographical study, a phenomenological study, or Action Research (which focuses on improving your practice).

In Part two of this book Dawn observes that:

> In order to select the most appropriate research method for this study it was essential to consider the features of both qualitative and quantitative methodologies. Quantitative research generates statistics through the use of large scale survey research or experiments. Qualitative research explores attitudes, behaviours and experiences (Dawson 2007, p25). Often the purpose of quantitative research is to test a theory or verify a claim using statistical data by being as objective as possible. (Qualitative research is subjective and is used to generate theories rather than verify them, using data describing attitudes, beliefs and feelings (Punch 2010, p57). … Qualitative methods have been selected due to the potential for extracting depth by exploring in detail the participants feelings and emotions on which the study is highly dependable. The researcher will be exploring individuals in her own line of work therefore an interpretivist approach is relevant as personal background and attitudes make it difficult for the researcher to see the situation from a purely neutral standpoint
>
> (Walliman and Buckler 2010).

Once you have decided on the most appropriate paradigm for your study, you need to select a methodology which is congruent with the paradigm (see the 'Research overview' at end of Part one of this book). One of the more common approaches is the 'case study'. A case study, according to

Punch (2014:120) "aims to understand the case in depth, and in its natural setting, recognizing its complexity and context". What constitutes a 'case' can be flexible, as long as it is in a bounded context. For instance, a case can focus on an individual or group of individuals, a school or setting, or any other organization, a city or town, or part of a country, an event or policy, etc. It is this flexibility which makes it such an attractive methodology for an educational research project. A perceived disadvantage of a case study is that due to its uniqueness, it is difficult to make any generalisations from it. At best, its findings can be related to other, maybe similar, situations.

No fewer than five out of the six proposals offered in Part two of this book employ a case study as their methodology.

Catherine explains that:

> *The methodology to be used is a case study research. Simons (2009, p.20) states there are a variety of definitions of case study with different emphases, although they all have in common the "commitment to studying a situation or phenomenon in it real life context, to understanding complexity" and be bounded by time, place and participants (Creswell, 2013b, p.494).*

Her case focuses on student perspectives (on mathematics) within their school environment. Julia concentrates on the opinions on homework of a specific group of students, namely those in Year 10 (of a particular school) with a view to gaining an insight into the factors and outside influences that may affect or prevent students from completing their homework. Lisa's case is the behaviour demonstrated by pupils in a Year Five class of a South of England Primary School, with regard to extrinsic motivational rewards. As demonstrated, cases can be varied, however, all are specific and bound by certain parameters.

Punch (2014:125) offers some guidelines for preparing a case study, which include:

- Be clear on what the case is and on what it is a case of

- Be clear on the need for the study and on the general purpose

- Translate this general purpose in specific research questions

- Show what data will be collected and how data will be analysed

An alternative to a case study approach can be a phenomenological study, as adopted by Dawn. She explains that:

> *The methodology used for this study will be the phenomenological approach. Phenomenology is particularly suited to small scale research where the main resource is the researcher. ...."It will try to provide a description of how things are experienced at first hand by those involved"*
>
> *(Denscombe 2010, p94).*

A phenomenological study, then, attempts to identify how an individual interprets phenomena through direct experience, which is then interpreted. It is concerned with the world of everyday life and is a most suitable approach within qualitative research. Dawn continues:

> *This could provide a valuable insight into Teaching Assistants own perspectives as to whether they are effective in their roles and if not how this could be addressed as part of their professional development.*

She further points out that:

> *There are disadvantages to the phenomenological approach in such that it lacks scientific emphasis. However in a study that is wholly focused on the ways in which people interpret events in order to make sense of their personal experience, a scientific quantitative approach would not extract the rich data that is required.*

Action Research is concerned with improving one's own practice. Although suitable as a methodology, it may not be relevant to full-time students of an Education programme. Furthermore, opportunities for those working in an educational setting may be limited, making it difficult to demonstrate research skills. Guidance on how to conduct Action Research and relevant exemplars can be found in one of our previous publications: Malthouse, R. & Roffey-Barentsen, J. (2013) *Action Research Projects: A Collection*. London: Thalassa Publishing.

Methodologies such as ethnography and grounded theory usually require more time to complete than is available for an undergraduate research project. They are rarely seen within this context and therefore not considered in this publication on Proposals.

Your next consideration is your 'sample', or who to gather the information from so you can answer your research question. In this type of research, as pointed out by Burton *et al.* (2008:46) "….samples are relatively small, but nevertheless have to be selected carefully from a total population". It is most likely that you decide on a strategy called 'non-probability sampling' to select the most appropriate participants for your research. Within this strategy you can employ methods such as 'purposive sampling', in which you use your own judgement in the selection of participants according to their characteristics. 'Convenience sampling' (or volunteer sampling) is where you select participants according to their ease of access (people you know, friends, colleagues, pupils you work with). This type of sampling may be easy to arrange, however, there are disadvantages with regard to representativeness. For instance asking your friends about a hobby you all share may give you a skewed outcome; therefore be cautious about this type of sampling. Further, you may consider a 'quota sample' in which you take into account the distribution of for instance gender, ethnicity, ability, etc of the larger population (if there are 30 girls and 20 boys in a year group, you may decide to select 3 girls and 2 boys for interview).

Catherine selected her sample as follows:

Two focus groups will be used formed from a convenience sample of six students; further, all female students currently in year 11 will be asked to complete the questionnaire, a sample size of 50. The focus groups will be comprised of students from classes the researcher teaches or supports.

Monica also opts for a convenience sample:

Convenience sampling (Roberts – Holmes, 2011) will be used here as, being a childminder myself I have easy access to two childminding groups spanning two separate counties. All members of the groups will be given a questionnaire and have the opportunity to participate, therefore no exclusions will be made from the population.

Gina offers:

Ary (2010, p.423) states that qualitative research "typically use purposive sampling". The questionnaire will be sent to all teachers within the organisation, apart from the Learning Support teachers as they have a different role and do not teach mainstream classes.

As explained, convenience sampling can be inappropriate; however, you must consider how you can gain access to the chosen population; therefore, an early enquiry would be sensible. It would also be helpful to identify the gatekeeper(s); whose permission do you need to gain access?

Methods of Data Collection

There are a number of ways in which you can collect data, or information, from your participants. The most commonly used in educational research are questionnaires, interviews, observations and documents/records. As is to be expected, each method has its strengths and limitations. It is up to you, the researcher, to decide on which method(s) will generate the best data in order to be able to answer your research question.

Monica has decided on a questionnaire as the best method of data collection for her research:

> *Questionnaires using the Likert scale method will be sent to approximately 30 childminders, gaining results of a numerical nature. Different scenarios will be presented as statements. There will only be 4 possible answers in each case, ranging from "strongly agree" to "strongly disagree", to eliminate the chance of all replies falling into the "not sure" area as this would make results inconclusive.*

> *Although the questionnaire will be using the Likert scale, it will be adapted to incorporate free text questions for childminders to give further information regarding opinions and attitudes. This will give results of a narrative nature as it will be gathering people's opinions.*

This adaption has been chosen as it was originally hoped to gather
information from a questionnaire, followed by a focus group to gather
further information. However, due to practical issues such as time,
venue, et cetera this will not be possible. By adding the free text
questions it is hoped to gather similar information. Therefore the
questionnaire will be made of both closed questions, with fixed
answers, and open questions in the free text boxes where a
participant will write their own answer.

Gina discusses her decisions on data collection as follows, demonstrating
an awareness of the limitations:

In order to answer the research question, the perspectives of
the teachers must be sought. The data will be gathered in the
form of a qualitative questionnaire, featuring open questions.

Cohen, Manion and Morrison (2011) suggest participants tend
to be more honest when answering questionnaires, due to their
anonymity. Walliman and Buckler (2008) declare the need for
clear and unambiguous language to be used in the
questionnaires as misunderstandings cannot be clarified. It is
therefore important to pilot the questionnaire. Thomas (2013)
warns of potentially low return rates. The researcher will email
a reminder to the participants during the data collection
process.

Piloting any form of data collection is important and should always be
considered for the reason given above. Lisa will also pilot her
questionnaire:

Initially, a pilot group will be invited to complete pilot questionnaires, enabling the researcher to ascertain if proposed questions will produce appropriate qualitative data to answer the research question. This reflects the beliefs of Cohen, Manion and Morrison (2011), which imply piloting chosen data collection methods highlight potential weaknesses, safeguard against question ambiguity and identify technical problems. Newby (2010) warns against the careless phrasing of questions, which could generate unwanted superfluous data. Ambiguous questions can then be rectified before the final questionnaire is distributed.

Gina continues, introducing a second method of data collection:

'Cohen, Manion and Morrison (2011) define methodological triangulation as using different methods of data collection. The views of a Teaching and Learning Consultant, who has been working with the school, will be sought....This will be in the form of a semi-structured interview. According to O'Hara et al (2011, p.171) semi-structured interviews allow themes and ideas relating to the research question to be explored, with the opportunity to ask probing questions to garner more detail. A framework of questions will be developed which are in line with the questions featured in the questionnaire in order to ensure that the interview remains valid and relevant. The interview will last for 30 minutes and will be recorded using an audio device.'

Julia has also selected semi structured interviews but she intends to conduct a number of individual interviews with specific participants. The limitations of interviews as a tool for data collection are also discussed:

The main focus of the research is to gather the opinions of the students. Therefore, in order to answer the research question effectively, the preferred method of data collection will be in the form of a semi structured interview. A semi structured interview is where the researcher will have a specific number of questions on the chosen topic, but has the freedom to elaborate and clarify the questions to the interviewee.

The interviews will be recorded using an audio recorder so as to ensure the researcher has an account of all of the students' responses given in the interviews. However, a disadvantage to recording interviews is that body language and facial expressions can obviously not be recorded, so therefore it is useful for the researcher to make notes on this during the interviews.

The research will take place within a year 10 maths class that the researcher supports in herself (…) As the aim of the research is to identify the reasons as to why some students regularly fail to complete their homework, the students that will be included in the interviews will be those (…) that repeatedly do not do their homework. Each student will be asked exactly the same questions by the researcher in the same format. The interviews will take place during the students' maths lesson so will not cause disruption to their school day.

There is a danger of researcher bias with this chosen method as the researcher is well known to the students. The students may not answer the questions truthfully for fear of upsetting the researcher. There is a possibility that their responses to the questions asked, will only reflect what they feel the researcher wants to hear rather than their true feelings. In contrast, the researcher as she knows the students well could also interpret their answers according to what she believes their perception of homework to be.

Dawn has opted for another type of interview: the group interview:

Group interviews will be used in this study as the only source of information due to their potential to provide detailed insight from teaching assistants perspectives about their own training and professional development. (...)   Due to the time consuming nature of collecting data from group interviews and the restraints on the size of group to ensure manageability, it will not be possible to interview the entire population of teaching assistants at each school (...) To gain meaningful data for this study the group must have experienced working with secondary school students with SEN. Therefore this sample will be small, consisting of three groups, one from each secondary school. Each group will consist of four teaching assistants (1 HLTA and 3 TA) who have been working in secondary school for a minimum of 6 months, have experience of supporting SEN students in an inclusive classroom setting and are willing to take part in the study.

As you will have noticed from the above, there is a range of methods to choose from when collecting data. Furthermore, there isn't one 'correct' method, to the exclusion of all others. Your decision, therefore, has to based upon which method, in your view, would generate the best data for you to be able to address your research question, taking into account the practicality of the method; in other words, will you be able to use that method, given the timeframe, sample, situation, etc. available to you. It would be appropriate, at this stage, to consider how you will record the data.

Methods of Data Analysis:

Once you have decided how you will collect your data and have considered what this data will look like – for instance, will there be a number of completed questionnaires, hours of recorded interviews or their transcripts, bundles of field notes or observations – you need to think of how to make sense of all this information. Therefore, you need to plan how you will analyse the data. In part two, Julia addresses issues of data analysis, citing Bryman, as she refers to data reduction:

> Bryman (2012, p13) explains that: "The data analysis stage is fundamentally about data reduction – that is, it is concerned with reducing the large corpus of information that the researcher has gathered so that he or she can make sense of it".

Although it may be tempting to wait until all the data has been gathered, before you start the analysis, there is no need for this; in fact, it may be better to begin analysing the data as soon as you collect it. Julia suggests that:

> The process of data analysis will commence during the data collection. In addition to the recordings of the interviews, the researcher will take notes of the non-verbal communication after each interview and produce a transcript to support the data analysis. Dawson (2012, p115) advises that to help with the analysis of qualitative data: "It is useful to produce an interview summary form which you complete as soon as possible after each interview has taken place. This includes practical details about the time and place, the participants, the duration of the interview and details of emerging themes".

Making appropriate links to the literature, Julia is describing the techniques she will employ during the data analysis. It is very easy to feel swamped by data unless it is suitably controlled. Following the data collection Julia observes:

> *After the interview process has been completed, the researcher will interpret the qualitative data that has been collected by using thematic analysis. Thematic data analysis involves grouping the data into themes or categories that are relevant to the research question. The researcher will look for patterns in the data and whether key words or terms are repeated throughout the interview process. Furthermore, the researcher will look to see whether any comparisons can be made between individual students' answers.*

Essentially, Julia's analysis will be that of thematic data analysis, where she is looking for themes that emerge from the data.

Catherine proposes a similar approach but also mentions 'coding' of data:

> *Open ended questions from the questionnaire will be highlighted to identify common themes (Cohen, Manion, and Morrison, 2011, p.537). Results from closed questions will be collated using an analysis sheet (Gillham, 2000, p.7). Data will then be disseminated and organised into common themes, which will require data to be coded to allow it to be easily identified with its original source (Layder, 2013, p130).*

Similarly, Gina offers the following when considering her data analysis:

> *Walliman and Buckler (2008) recommend a process of coding whereby the results are reduced into a table of keywords, within which a tally*

can be created. It is likely that the questionnaires will arrive over a period of time so the data will subjected to what Ary (2010, p.425) terms "inductive analysis". The data will be coded as it arrives so that the researcher is constantly interpreting and categorising. The transcript from the consultant interview will use the same coding system to enable comparison, although it will be highlighted to mark it as distinct from the teacher participants.

Although most students prefer analysing their data manually, there is a range of software packages available which may be of help.

Validity, reliability and generalisability

As pointed out by Burton *et al.* (2008) validity, reliability and generalisability are the quality criteria commonly associated with traditional research. Validity refers to the integrity of the research: is there internal consistency; do the findings reflect what has been studied. To enhance validity there are a few strategies you can consider. As seen earlier, piloting your questionnaire or interview schedule will help to ensure the questions asked are relevant to the research question, clear and unambiguous. Also, you may want to ask a 'critical friend' to check your analysis and conclusions. Further, you could consider 'respondent validity' or 'member checking', a strategy which asks the participants to confirm their contributions (by asking them to check the transcript, for instance). Triangulation, which means gathering data from different sources by employing two or more methods of data collection, is also a strategy used to increase validity. The discussion of these strategies in your proposal demonstrates your forward thinking and robust approach to conducting research.

Reliability refers to the consistency of the research; will you be able to replicate it, using the same methods, asking the same participants, but on a different occasion. Also, will other researchers, using those methods, asking those participants, generate the same responses? If reliable, it may then be possible to generalise from the research, making some generic claims. Burton *et al.* (2008:168), however, highlight that reliability and generalisability are: "difficult, if not impossible to fulfill by qualitative researchers undertaking small-scale investigations..." It is important that you acknowledge this at the planning stage of your research by stating its limitations in terms of generalisability. It is recognized that in qualitative research notions such as 'authenticity', 'trustworthiness', and 'transferability' of the research may be more appropriate. Again, it is important that you consider these issues at the proposal stage of the research.

Lisa strives for the validity of her research:

> *To ensure validity, this study will have clear correlations between qualitative data collected and the research question.*

Monica considers piloting her questionnaire:

> *Piloting the questionnaire should increase the internal validity as it will show up any flaws in its design, checking that the questions address the research question. Cohen et al (2011:183) describe internal validity as "the findings... must describe accurately the phenomena being researched."*

Lisa, however, is aware that reliability is unlikely:

> *Qualitative research, involving people's interpretations of the world (Bell, 2010), can by its very nature, Creswell (1998) suggests, be valid*

yet unreliable......

However, to be deemed reliable, Bell (2010) suggests, research must be replicable and repeatable. Other researchers should be able to perform exactly the same research under the same conditions, generating the same results and not simply a one-off. Consequently, as raffle tickets (only displaying dates and subjects) are awarded to pupils at various times throughout the school day by different teachers, exactly the same conditions would not be replicable (Cohen, Manion and Morrison, 2011).

Ethical Considerations

It is imperative that you consider the ethics of your research; after all, you have a 'duty of care in relation to all those participating in the research process' (Burton *et al*, 2008:50). Your institution may even have an 'Ethics Committee' which decides whether you may continue with your research. So, what constitutes this duty of care? The British Educational Research Association (BERA)(2011) has published guidance for researchers, which includes responsibilities to participants of the research, such as the need for anyone who is involved in the research to be treated with respect; for them to be treated fairly, sensitively, with dignity and with freedom from prejudice. Most researchers offer their participants confidentiality and anonymity, so they cannot be identified by third parties. All participants should understand what the research is about, achieved by a 'participant information sheet', and they should agree to participate voluntarily. Researchers will usually ask their participants to sign a consent form, which provides evidence of participants' voluntary informed consent. Furthermore, researchers must inform their participants of the right to withdraw from the research, at any stage, without having to give a reason. Research which involves children or vulnerable people may require you to get the consent of parents, guardians or significant others.

Lisa considers the subject of ethics where she draws the reader's attention to the 'BERA guidelines':

> *This study will adhere to British Ethical Research Association (BERA) ethical guidelines by maintaining participants' anonymity (BERA, 2011), which Creswell (1998) suggests, can be further protected by assigning numbers to participants' questionnaires…..*

Issues of consent and gate keepers are next considered, as she observes that:

> *Prior to the study commencing, overall consent will be obtained from the headteacher (gatekeeper). Bell (2010) suggests, as the study will occur within normal day-to-day school routines and not involve the pupils directly, pupil-parent consent will not be required (Newby, 2010), as the headteacher's overall consent will be adequate (BERA, 2011).*

Anonymity and nonparticipation were discussed, with Lisa feeling that:

> *It was felt that the ethical implications of questionnaires would be most appropriate at protecting participants' anonymity. Questionnaires will inform participants of the study's aim, requirements, data usage, rights to comment upon the results and receive feedback upon completion (Newby, 2010). Participants will be notified of their rights to anonymity, nonparticipation (Nuremberg Code, 1949) and withdrawal from*

the study at any given time (Greig and Taylor, 1999).

Gina employs a different approach to consent:

> *The teachers will be contacted via email which will contain the consent information. This will take the form of "implied consent" (Thomas, 2013, p.49) whereby the participants will be informed that it will be assumed that they agree to taking part in the research unless they specifically email the researcher to decline.*

Ensuring data is securely stored, Lisa explains that:

> *Data will be collected and securely stored in locked cupboards. Once completed and submitted …., the ethical implications determine all study data and documents will be destroyed (BERA, 2011).*

In general, when planning your research, you must consider all the ethical issues with regard to your research.

References

To demonstrate evidence of your wider reading, supporting your arguments and decisions made, you have to accurately cite and reference your sources. The 'citing' happens in the text, as you make use of direct quotes or refer to someone's writing. The 'referencing' is at the end of the work, listing your sources. Although there are different systems for citing and referencing, such as author-date systems or numerical ones using footnotes, the one most commonly used in educational research is the Harvard system. Do check, however, with your tutors which system you should adopt. Pears and Shields (2013) offer clear, detailed advice on citing and referencing and we recommend you consult their publication.

This concludes the elements of an educational research proposal. By following these steps systematically you will cover all that is required for a successful proposal. The next part of this publication offers the largely unedited proposals of some Education Studies students, giving you a further insight into how to approach your proposal.

References

British Educational Research Association (2011) *Ethical Guidelines for Educational Research.* Available online at https://www.bera.ac.uk [Accessed 22/09/2015]

Burton, N., Brundrett, M. & Jones, M. (2008*) Doing your Education Research Project*. London: Sage Publications Ltd.

Cohen, L., Manion, L. & Morrison, K. (2000) *Research Methods in Education.* 5th Edn. London: Routledge Falmer.

Pears, R. & Shields, G. (2013) Cite them right: the essential referencing guide. London: Palgrave MacMillan

Punch, K. (2014) *Introduction to Social Research*. London: Sage Publications Ltd.

Please note that citations used in the extracts above are referenced in the individual proposals in part two.

Research overview

Paradigm	Overarching perspective concerning appropriate research practice based on ontological and epistemological assumptions	Positivist	Interpretivist
Ontology	Assumptions about nature of reality What is reality	The truth is 'out there', regardless of us Objective	Truth is constructed by us Subjective
Epistemology	Assumptions about what we can know about reality, what is the relationship between knowledge and reality How is knowledge created	Meaning exists in the world Knowledge reflects reality	Meaning exists in our interpretations of the world Knowledge is interpretation

Methodology	Specifies how the researcher may go about studying what (s)he believes can be known How can we investigate reality	Experimental Survey	Case Study Action Research Phenomenology Ethnography Grounded Theory
Methods of data collection	How to collect data	Experiments Tests Questionnaires Documents Structured interviews	Interviews Focus groups Observation Field notes Diaries/ documents
Nature of data	What does the data look like	Quantitative	Qualitative

Part two: Exemplars

This part of the publication contains six exemplar research proposals. We anticipate that by reading these proposals, focusing on the structure and general approach, you will get a good idea of how to fashion your proposal. The students who have contributed their work briefly introduce themselves, allowing you to get a better understanding of why they have engaged in the research.

1. CATHERINE FRANCIS

I work as a Higher Level Teaching Assistant in the Mathematics Department of a secondary school in Hampshire and am studying for a BA (Hons) Education. I work with students aged 11-16 years with a range of abilities and special educational needs. When selecting the topic for my Research Project I decided to concentrate on perceptions of Mathematics from a girl's viewpoint, specifically relating to whether they would continue with the topic at Sixth Form College.

Title

A case study exploring girls' perceptions of progressing to post–16 mathematics studies.

Research question

What are girls' perceptions of continuing with mathematics beyond GCSE level?

Introduction

The purpose of this research project is to explore the factors that contribute to the lack of girls' post-16 participation in mathematics. The researcher has chosen this topic as "the mathematical skill gap" has been highlighted as "a problem which had become acute" affecting students wishing to study Science, Technology, Engineering and Mathematics (STEM) degrees (Select Committee on Science and Technology, 2012), and by employers who identified a shortage of students with adequate maths skills (CBI, 2011, p.6/7). A previous report by Smith (2004, p.13) also made reference to the need for students to "continue longer with the study of mathematics".

Since 2005 there has been a year on year increase in entries for AS mathematics (Department for Education (DfE), 2011, p.26). Statistics also show "high prior attaining boys are even more likely than their female counterparts to enter A level maths" (Great Britain. DfE, 2011, p.115). Research by Mendick (2005) and Cann (2009) state higher proportions of boys choose AS mathematics than girls.

This research project will explore the affect of gender, prior attainment, and planned participation in post-16 mathematics of students from a Hampshire secondary school, which has been judged by Ofsted (2012) as preparing students well "for the next phase of their education".

Literature Review

No research project "stands on its own" (Lambert, 2012, p79). A literature review allows the researcher to gain knowledge of the topic chosen (Anderson and Arsenault, 1998, p.76), developing an understanding of research already written. By identifying key issues the researcher will give "credibility and legitimacy to the research" (Cohen, Manion, and Morrison, 2011, p.112).

The literature review will initially look at the importance of participation in post-16 mathematics. It will review the affect of attainment using the DfE literature and the findings of the TIMSS 2011 assessment. The main focus of the review will be to explore the key issues influencing girls' participation in mathematics beyond GCSE level. The findings will be used as a "platform" for the research project (Greetham, 2009, p.240).

Methodology

The starting point for this research project is the ontology, how the reality is constructed, defined as "the nature of reality" (Cohen, Manion, and Morrison, 2011, p.33 and Creswell, 2013a, p.20) further explained as "multiple realities exist and are dependent on the individual" (Guba, 1996, cited by Denzin and Lincoln, 2011, p.102). Creswell (2013a, p.20) states "different researchers embrace different realities". For this research project the researcher will report "these multiple realities" by pranesenting the findings of all perspectives and the subjective realities of students participating.

Epistemology defined as "what counts as knowledge and how knowledge claims are justified" (Creswell, 2013a, p.20) therefore how significant is knowledge gained and "how we come to know these multiple realities" (Cohen, Manion, and Morrison, 2011, p.33). Guba and Lincoln (1985, cited by Denzin and Lincoln, 2011, p.102) state meaning and understanding is constructed through "interaction with our surrounding" this will be specific to the individual.

Denzin and Lincoln, (2011, p.12) and Creswell (2013a, p.21) emphasise the importance of the relationship between researcher and participants whereby the researcher becomes an insider enriching their understanding of the perceived realties. The epistemological assumption will require the collection of subjective evidence "based on individual views" (Creswell, 2013a, p.20). This should occur within the student environment as this will give context to the knowledge gained as recommended by Creswell (2013a, p.20).

The paradigm, "models, perspectives or conceptual frameworks that help to organize our thoughts, beliefs, views and practices" (Basit, 2010, p.14). This research project will be an interpretive paradigm based on ontological and epistemological assumptions as defined by Cohen, Manion, and Morrison, (2011, p.17) "to understand the subjective world of human experience" as it will analysis perceptions and interpret the reality subjectively as viewed by individual students (Basit, 2010, p.14 and Denzin and Lincoln, 2011, p.102). In so doing it will investigate student perspectives within their school environment (Gray, 2009, p.27) and reflect their view point within the research project (Cohen, Manion, and

Morrison, 2011, p.17).

The methodology to be used is a case study research. Simons (2009, p.20) states there are a variety of definitions of case study with different emphases, although they all have in common the "commitment to studying a situation or phenomenon in it real life context, to understanding complexity" and be bounded by time, place and participants (Creswell, 2013b, p.494).

Case study research has been chosen as it enables the researcher to "interpret the uniqueness of real individuals and situations through accessible accounts" (Cohen, Manion, and Morrison, 2011, p.129) and allow a deeper analysis of student perception than would be apparent from numerical analysis (Cohen, Manion, and Morrison, 2011, p.129 and Thomas, 2011, p.7). This will be achieved using a variety of "sources of evidence" (Yin, 1984, p.23). The use of triangulation improves validity; reduces the possibility of bias and highlights any inconsistency within the data (Mathison, 1988, p13-15). It also enriches "research findings" (Gillham, 2000, p.102) and will "increase the credibility" of knowledge gained (Hussein, 2009, p.10). This is particularly important in a case study as one of the recognised disadvantages is researcher bias due to researcher involvement in the study (Cohen, Manion, and Morrison, 2011, p.290, Flyvbjerg, 2006, p234 and Yin 2013, p.76).

Advantages of case study research is the ability acknowledge the differences between viewpoints (Adelman et al (1980) cited Cohen, Manion, and Morrison, 2011, p.292) and are able to be complete by one researcher (Nisbet and Watt cited Cohen, Manion, and Morrison, 2011, p.292 and Yin, 2013, p.72)

Methods of data collection

Data from the school and its associated further education college will be requested from the school and college administrators, analysed and used to identify whether this is an actual issue for girls' attending the school. This data will include GCSE mathematics results for the previous four years with relevant key stage 3 results for each year group, and the predicted GCSE grade and the key stage 3 results for the current year group.

To ensure there is sufficient data available to analyse student perceptions; a focus group and questionnaire will be used as data collection methods. Two focus groups will be used formed from a convenience sample of six students; further, all female students currently in year 11 will be asked to complete the questionnaire, a sample size of 50.

The focus groups will be comprised of students from classes the researcher teaches or supports. The screening process used will be to identify those who have chosen not to continue with mathematics post-16 and are willing to participate (Vaughn, Schumm and Sinagub, 1996, p.64). To avoid disruption uncooperative students or close friends will not be selected as this may affect the spontaneity of the discussion (Morgan, 1988, p.42 and Reed and Payton, 1997, p.766). The number of students taking part will be restricted to three as the focus group discussion will be time limited, to allow all students to contribute fully in the discussion (Krueger and Casey, 2008, p.15).

The use of focus groups has been chosen as the aim is to facilitate discussion amongst participants using focus materials, collect student opinion and viewpoints (Thomas, 2011, p.7 and Tonkiss, 2004, p.194). The role of the researcher will be to "listen and gather information" (Krueger and Casey, 2008, p.2). Yin (2013, p.110) and Krueger and Casey, (2008, p.2 and 36) recommend using friendly and non threatening questions for interviews and this will be applied to the materials and questions chosen to encourage spontaneous participation. Open ended questions are recommended as they reveal what the interviewee is thinking rather than the interviewer (Krueger and Casey, 2008, p.54).

Litosseliti (2003, p.18-27) states another advantage of using focus groups is to gain qualitative primary data including the "views, attitudes, beliefs, responses, motivations and perceptions" of participants. Comments from one participant can lead to a "snowballing" effect as additional comments follow from the other students and the group can become excited by the topic, this is known as "stimulation" (Vaughn, Schumm and Sinagub, 1996, p.14).

Disadvantages include researcher bias, as participants may feel they need to agree with the researcher's opinion if given. Quiet students will be hindered in communicating their views due to the dominances of other students in the group and be unwilling to disagree with group views (Litosseliti, 2003, p.18). Careful planning of questions, materials and moderating of the discussion will be needed to reduce these risks (Litosseliti, 2003, p.27, Mauthner, 1997, p.21 and Krueger and Casey, 2008, p.15). Themes and topics generated by the focus groups will later be used in the creation of the questionnaire (Cohen, Manion, and Morrison, 2011, p.436, Litosseliti, 2003, p.27 and Krueger and Casey, 2008, p.15). Critical incidences will be recorded in a focus group diary to support transcription (Krueger and Casey, 2008, p.126 and Vaughn, Schumm and Sinagub, 1996, p.101).

Questionnaires are an efficient use of time as a large number of students can be asked their perceptions (Munn and Drever, 1990, p.2), being cost effective (Strange et al, 2003, p.337), and as students understand the procedure they are usually willing to complete them (Lambert, 2012, p.102). A further benefit is that data collected will relate directly to the case study which will be achieved by meticulous composition, including examining questionnaires previously used in educational research (Newby, p.337).

It will be structured to collect qualitative and quantitative data (Lambert, 2012, p.102). To avoid "research fatigue" it will be constructed to capture student interest and reduce the burden on the class teacher by being as concise as possible whilst still collecting the required data (Felzmann, 2009, p.107 and Brace, 2013, p.8). Participants will be given time to complete the questionnaire to improve response rates (Lambert, 2012, p.103 and Cohen, Manion, and Morrison, 2011, p.404).

Initially a pilot questionnaire will be used to provide evidence of question clarity (Gillham, 2000, p.19), increase reliability and validity (Cohen, Manion, and Morrison, 2011, p.402) and enable a full range of responses to be collected (Cohen, Manion, and Morrison, 2011, p.381). To minimise the number of open questions a range of responses to individual questions will be identified by the focus groups and pilot questionnaires (Gillham, 2000, p.63). As the researcher would like individual and therefore personal perceptions from students they will be encouraged to complete the questionnaire on their own (Strange et al, 2003, p.337).

Methods of data analysis

The analysis of quantitative data will involve counting, separating out, and comparing the information collected (Lambert, 2012, p.163). Comparisons of data will be descriptive, reporting factually the information gathered (Cohen, Manion, and Morrison, 2011, p.606) and identify relationships (Greetham, 2009, p.227 Langdride and Hagger-Johnson, 2013, p.165).

The analysis of qualitative data will commence after deciding which data is relevant to the research question (Greetham, 2009, p.227 and Cohen, Manion, and Morrison, 2011, p.537). The focus group conversations will be transcribed as soon as possible after the meeting (Greetham, 2009, p.226). Open ended questions from the questionnaire will be highlighted to identify common themes (Cohen, Manion, and Morrison, 2011, p.537). Results from closed questions will be collated using an analysis sheet (Gillham, 2000, p.7). Data will then be disseminated and organised into common themes, which will require data to be coded to allow it to be easily identified with its original source (Layder, 2013, p130).

Validity/ Reliability

Validity defined as "the extent to which an instrument helps a researcher to find out what she or he wishes to find out" (Lambert, 2012, p.135) and requires data collection methods to provide answers to the research question. Reliability defined as "a method is free from error. When it is used repeatedly, it produces consistent results" (Lambert, 2012, p.136).

The use of both focus groups and a questionnaire as a form of triangulation will strengthen the validity of the research project by compensating for weakness in either method. (Lambert, 2012, p.138 and Layder, 2013, p.91). To ensure internal validity of the completed research project explanations will be supported transparently with evidence from the data (Cohen, Manion, and Morrison, 2011, p.295).

When replicated the results of the focus groups may not be consistent as prior experiences of participants and interpretation by the researcher may cause different outcomes. As the research ontological and epistemological assumptions are interpretive all data collected will be valid as these reflect the realities of those participants (Cohen, Manion, and Morrison, 2011, p.295).

Inferences made from one focus group are not recommended (Vaughn, Schumm and Sinagub, 1996, p.60) therefore two focus groups will be used to strengthen data reliability. Participants will be asked to validate transcripts and the subsequent questionnaire to ensure they reflect the student perceptions (Torrance, 2012, p.4).

Ethical Considerations

British Educational Research Association (BERA) (2011, p.5) states "Individuals should be treated fairly, sensitively, with dignity, and within an ethic of respect". Ethical consideration begins at the start of the research project and will be achieved by informing the head teacher acting as "loco parentis" (Felzmann, 2009, p.105), staff and students of the purpose, methods of data collection and future use (BERA, 2011, p.5-6, and Layder, 2013, p.16). Informed consent will be requested from all participants with the assurance of "confidentiality and anonymity" (BERA, 2011, p.7 and Layder, 2013, p.118). This will only be breached if necessary under "child protection legislation" (Felzmann, 2009, p.106). All participants will have the right to withdraw and the best interest of participants will be considered continuously throughout the research project (BERA, 2011, p.6, and Layder, 2013, p.17). Age appropriate language, materials and explanations will be used (Felzmann, 2009, p.104 and Mauthner, 1997, p.18).

All data collected will be "stored securely" and the final report will not breach "confidentiality and anonymity" (BERA, 2000, p.8). When writing the final report "academic integrity" will be respected to ensure the findings are made accurately without distortion or bias (BERA, 2000, p.4) and shared with those who participated in the research project (Felzmann, 2009, p.107).

References

Anderson, G. and Arsenault, N. (1998) *Fundamentals of Educational Research,* London. RoutledgeFalmer

Basit, T.N. (2010) *Conducting Research in Educational Contexts*. London Continuum International Publishing Group.

BERA (British Educational Research Association) (2011) *Ethical guidelines for educational research.* [Online] Available at: http://www.bera.ac.uk/about/who-we-are (Accessed 13 November 2013).

BERA (British Educational Research Association) (2000) *Good practice in Educational research writing* [Online] Available at:
www.**bera**.ac.uk/system/files/3/**BERA**-Ethical-Guidelines-2011 (Accessed 13 November 2013).

Brace, I. (2013) *Questionnaire design: How to plan structure and write survey material for effective market research* 3rd ed. London. Kogan Page.

CBI (2011), *Building for growth business priorities for education and skills, Educations and skills survey 2011.* [Online]. Available at:
http://www.cbi.org.uk/media/1051530/cbi__edi_education__skills_survey_2011.pdf (Accessed 30 September 2013)

Cohen, L. Manion, L. and Morrison, K. (2011) *Research Methods in Education.* 7th ed. London: Routledge.

Creswell, J.W. (2013a) *Qualitative Inquiry and Research design: Choosing among five approaches.* 3rd Ed. London. Sage Publications

Creswell, J.W. (2013b) *Educational research: planning, conducting, and evaluating quantitative and qualitative research* 4th ed. [e-book] Harlow: Pearson. Available at:
http://lib.myilibrary.com?id=526970&entityid=https://idp.farn-ct.ac.uk/idp/shibboleth (Accessed 5 November 2013).

Denzin, N.K. and Lincoln, Y.S. (2011) *The Sage Handbook of Qualitative Research.* 4th Ed. London. Sage Publications

Felzmann, H. (2009) Ethical issues in school based research. *Research Ethics Review.* Vol 5(3) [Online]. Available at:
http://rea.sagepub.com/content/5/3/104.full.pdf+html (Accessed 5 November

2013)

Flyvbjerg, B. (2006) Five Misunderstandings about Case-Study Research. *Qualitative Inquiry.* Vol12 (2) [Online]. Available at: http://qix.sagepub.com/content/12/2/219 (Accessed 5 November 2013)

Gillham, B. (2000) *Developing a questionnaire (Real world research).* London Continuum International Publishing Group.

Gray, D.E. (2009) *Doing Research in the Real World.* 2nd ed. London. Sage Publications.

Great Britain. Department for Education (2011), *Maths and Science education: the supply of high achievers at A level.* [Online]. Available at: https://www.gov.uk/government/publications/maths-and-science-education-the-supply-of-high-achievers-at-a-level (Accessed 29 September 2013)

Greetham, B. (2009) *Palgrave Study Skills: How to write your undergraduate Dissertation.* Basingstoke Palgrave Macmillan

Grix, J. (2002) Introducing Students to the Generic Terminology of Social Research. *Politics* Vol 22 (3) pp.175-186 [Online]. Available at: http://onlinelibrary.wiley.com/doi/10.1111/1467-9256.00173/full (Accessed 31 October 2013)

Hussein, A. (2009)The use of Triangulation in Social Sciences Research: Can qualitative and quantitative methods be combined? *Journal of Comparative Social Work* Vol 1[Online] Available at: http://jcsw.no/local/media/jcsw/docs/jcsw_issue_2009_1_8_article.pdf (Accessed 5 November 2013)

Krueger, R. A. and Casey, M. A. (2008) Focus Groups: A practical Guide for Applied Research 4th ed. London Sage.

Lambert, M. (2012) *A beginner's guide to doing your education research project.* London: Sage Publications Ltd

Langdridge, D. and Hagger-Johnson, G. *Introduction to Research methods and analysis in psychology. 3rd* ed. Harlow Pearson Education

Layder, D. 2013, *Doing excellent small scale research.* London Sage

Litosseliti (2003) *Using focus groups in research.* London Continuum

Mauthner, M. (1997) Methodological aspects of collecting data from children: Lessons from three research projects. *Children and Society.* Vol 11 pp.16 -28 [Online]. Available at: http://onlinelibrary.wiley.com/doi/10.1111/j.1099-0860.1997.tb00003.x (Accessed 13 November 2013)

Mathison, S. (1988) Why Triangulate? *Educational Researcher.* [Online]. Available at: http://blogs.ubc.ca/qualresearch/files/2008/01/why-tirangulate.pdf (Accessed 5 November 2013)

Mendick, H. (2005) Mathematical stories: why do more boys than girls choose to study mathematics at AS-level in England? *British Journal of Sociology of Education* Vol 26(2) pp. 235-251 [Online]. Available at: http://dx.doi.org/10.1080/0142569042000294192 (Accessed 8 October 2013)

Morgan, D.L. (1988) *Focus groups as Qualitative Research.* London, Sage.

Munn, P. and Drever, E. (1990) *Using Questionnaires in small scale research. A teachers guide.* Edinburgh Scottish Council for Research in Education [Online]. Available http://files.eric.ed.gov/fulltext/ED326488.pdf (Accessed 6 November

2013)

Newby, P. (2010) *Research methods for Education.* Harlow Pearson Education Limited.

Ofsted (2012), *Inspection Report: Cranbourne Business and Enterprise College.* [Online]. Available at:

http://www.cranbourne.hants.sch.uk/Websites/cranbourne/images/Ofsted/Ofsted _Feb_2012/Cranbourne_Business_and_Enterprise_College_Report_WF7649783.pd f (Accessed 5 October 2013)

Reed, J. and Payton, V.R. (1997) Focus groups: issues of analysis and interpretation. *Journal of Advanced Nursing*, Vol 26, pp765–771[Online]. Available at:

http://onlinelibrary.wiley.com/doi/10.1046/j.1365-2648.1997.00395.x (Accessed 5 October 2013)

Select Committee on Science and Technology (2012), *Second report Higher Education in Science, Technology, Engineering and Mathematics (STEM) subjects.* London: HMSO. [Online]. Available at:

www.publications.parliament.uk/pa/ld201213/ldselect/ldsctech/37/3706.htm#n22 (Accessed 30 September 2013)

Simons, H. (2009) *Case study research in practice.* London. Sage Publications Inc.

Smith, A. (2004), *Making Mathematics Count*. London. The Stationary Office. [Online]. Available at:

http://www.mathsinquiry.org.uk/report/MathsInquiryFinalReport.pdf (Accessed 5 October 2013)

Strange, V. Forest, S. Oakley, A. and The Ripple Study Team. (2003) Using Research questionnaires with young people in school: the influence of the social context. *International Journal of Social Research Methodology* [Online]. Available at:

http://www.tandfonline.com/doi/pdf/10.1080/1364557021000024749 (Accessed 4 November 2013)

Thomas, G. (2011) *How to do your case study: A guide for students and Researchers*. London, Sage

Tonkiss, F. (2004) Using focus groups. In C. Seale, ed. (2004) *Researching Society and Culture*. London. Sage. pp.194-207

Torrance, H. (2012) Triangulation, respondent validation, and democratic participation in mixed methods research. *Journal of Mixed Methods Research* [Online]. Available at:

http://mmr.sagepub.com/content/early/2012/02/16/1558689812437185.full.pdf+ html   (Accessed 13 November 2013)

Vaughn, S. Schumm, J.S. and Sinagub, J.M. (1996) *Focus group interviews in Education and Psychology*. London, Sage

Yin, R.K. (1984) *Case Study Research. Design and Methods* [e-book] London Sage Publications. Available at Google Books

http://books.google.co.uk/books?id=bA1HAAAAMAAJ&focus=searchwithinvolume &q=empirical+inquiry+   (Accessed 4 November 2013)

Yin, R.K. (2013) *Case Study Research. Design and Methods*. 5th ed.London Sage Publications.

2. DAWN MILLS

Dawn Mills is an experienced Teaching Assistant (TA) with 6years primary school experience and 8 months experience in a mainstream secondary school, holding NVQ3 and Foundation Degree qualifications in teaching and learning support and currently working towards her BA (Hons) in Education. In May 2013 Dawn started working with SEN students in a mainstream secondary school where 25% of students are SEN/EAL. The challenging nature of the new role led the researcher to consider the following: How can those teaching assistants in mainstream secondary schools who are employed with limited previous experience or knowledge and skills in supporting the diverse needs of SEN students be effective in their role? What knowledge and skills would help TA improve their support and how could these needs be addressed as part of TA professional development and used towards career progression? These considerations went on to form the basis of the research project undertaken as part of Dawn's work towards achieving the BA (Hons) in Education.

Title

An exploration into the professional development needs of Teaching Assistants supporting students with Special Educational Needs (SEN) in mainstream secondary schools

Introduction

The number of Teaching Assistants have increased dramatically. Between 1999-2001 funding was made available to recruit 20000 teaching assistants for primary and secondary schools and provide induction training for them, (HMI 2002). Some identify this partly as a result of inclusion.

"the rise in the numbers of teaching assistants working in mainstream schools mirrors schools' and LEAs' growing commitment towards inclusion." (Balshaw and Farrell, 2002:4)

Roffey Barentsen (2012) refers to the National curriculum for schools (DfEE 1999) which states that learning should be challenging and relevant achieved by setting suitable learning challenges, responding to diverse learning needs of pupils and overcoming potential barriers to learning. The role of the teaching assistant is paramount in supporting students learning in order for schools and teachers to adhere to these principles.

"teaching assistants are there to provide the support to allow pupils with SEN to progress in a mainstream setting."

(Roffey Barentsen 2012p22)

In 2009 the Deployment and Impact of Support Staff (DISS) project questioned the effectiveness of teaching assistants. This research led the researcher to consider the following: How can Teaching Assistants, employed with limited previous experience or knowledge and skills in supporting teaching/learning, learning,difficulties and behavioural emotional and social difficulties, be effective in their support of secondary school SEN students with a wide range of needs? What knowledge and skills would help Teaching Assistants to improve their support and how could this be addressed as part of their professional development and used towards career progression?

Prior to Teeman et al (2009) and Blatchford et al (2009) large scale studies and Roffey-Barentsen (2012) small scale qualitative study, research was limited in the area of training and development of secondary school Teaching Assistants specifically. Evidence was limited on, the qualifications held, the training and development activities undertaken and their own perceptions regarding training. In addition, their views on the future roles to be played by teaching assistants in secondary schools and the employment and deployment profiles of these specific Teaching Assistants are also areas worthy of further research.

Research question

What are the professional development needs of teaching assistants supporting students with Special Educational Needs in secondary schools?

Aims and objectives

The aim is, defined by Walliman and Buckler (2010p63) as "the overarching purpose of the research," is to discover, explore and understand the training and professional development that Teaching Assistants feel is required to support SEN students in a mainstream secondary school effectively.

The objectives of the study are :

- to systematically explore the issue of the training and development needs of Teaching Assistants in secondary schools by undertaking an extensive literature review
- to explore differing perspectives regarding the skills, knowledge and working practices that teaching assistants feel are required to effectively support secondary students with SEN and examine Teaching Assistants motivation to develop professionally, by conducting focus group/interviews in 3 mainstream secondary schools in Surrey
- to analyse, then synthesize the differing perspectives in an attempt to propose suggestions for professional development

Literature Review

Literature will be reviewed regarding teaching assistant's background and experience, how it is developed and deployed. Also, personal qualities and attributes required.

Literature relating to the multitude of support needs will be reviewed to establish whether it is realistic for Teaching Assistants to be trained across such a broad spectrum.

Motivation to develop, qualifications and support available to teaching assistants will be researched along with workplace learning, mentoring and continuous professional development.

Methodology

In order to select the most appropriate research method for this study it was essential to consider the features of both qualitative and quantitative methodologies. Quantitative research generates statistics through the use of large scale survey research or experiments. Qualitative research explores attitudes, behaviours and experiences (Dawson 2007p25). Often the purpose of quantitative research is to test a theory or verify a claim using statistical data by being as objective as possible. Qualitative research is subjective and is used to generate theories rather than verify them, using data describing attitudes, beliefs and feelings. (Punch 2010p57)

This study will examine Teaching Assistants personal perspectives of their role in secondary schools and the training that they feel is required to be effective. This type of research is highly qualitative and therefore whilst trying to be valid it may not always be reliable. This is because "it is virtually impossible to replicate a social setting" Denscombe (2010p298). These issues result from applying the ontological stance that reality will be subjective in approach (Kidd et al 2003).

In order to demonstrate the reliability of qualitative research Seal et al (1999) and Lincoln and Guba (1985) agree that there is a need to demonstrate that research reflects procedures and decisions that readers can see and evaluate. In effect the process must be open for audit. This will be achieved in this study by documenting the research design process.

Qualitative methods have been selected due to the potential for extracting depth by exploring in detail the participants feelings and emotions on which the study is highly dependable. The researcher will be exploring individuals in her own line of work therefore an interpretivist approach is relevant as personal background and attitudes make it difficult for the researcher to see the situation from a purely neutral standpoint (Walliman and Buckler 2010). This will be considered when reviewing the research findings by ensuring that the research question is at the forefront of every decision made.

The methodology used for this study will be the phenomenological approach. Phenomenology is particularly suited to small scale research where the main resource is the researcher. In depth semi structured interviews will investigate and try to understand the thinking of teaching assistants in relation to the many different aspects of their role and the training that is required in order to be effective in the support of SEN students in schools.

> "It will try to provide a description of how things are experienced at first hand by those involved."
>
> (Denscombe 2010p94)

This could provide a valuable insight into Teaching Assistants own perspectives as to whether they are effective in their roles and if not how this could be addressed as part of their professional development.

There are disadvantages to the phenomenological approach in such that it lacks scientific emphasis. However in a study that is wholly focused on the ways in which people interpret events in order to make sense of their personal experience a scientific quantitative approach would not extract the rich data that is required.

Methods of data collection

"Qualitative researchers in education study spoken and written representation and records of human experience"

(Punch 2009p144)

Interviews are the most prominent data collection tool in qualitative research. They enable the researcher to access perceptions, meanings and definitions of situations and are a powerful way of understanding others (Punch 2009).

"Interviews provided a depth of information that you just can't get from a questionnaire"   (Coles and McGrath 2010p103)

For this study, data and information will be gathered qualitatively from a purposive sample of teaching assistants using semi-structured group interviews, in the form of focus groups. Interviews have been chosen due to the rich data that they are able to extract. Participants will be questioned on their background, induction training received, the learning needs of students, and whether they are equipped to provide appropriate support for those needs and be effective in this support. If they feel that they are ineffective, what do they need to become effective in their support of secondary school students? Their motivation to develop professionally and the support available to do this will also be researched.

Fontana and Frey (1994) classified individual and group interviews as either structured, semi structured or unstructured relating to the degree of depth and structure in the interview. With structured being at one end of the continuum, using pre-established questions with pre-set response categories, the interview does not go into any depth. In contrast unstructured interviews are not pre planned, with general questions to get the interview started and follow up questions emerging as the interview unfolds. Semi-structured interviews were felt to be the most appropriate in this case due to their use of specific interview questions as a starting point, whilst being open to the unexpected where relevant (Coles and McGrath 2010).

When selecting the type of interview to use it was important to consider exactly what it is that the study is looking to explore and the individuals that are going to be interviewed. King and Horrocks (2010p61) suggest that group interviews are able to gain opinions and attitudes at another level. This is consistent with the view of Blumer,

> "A small number of individuals, brought together as a discussion or resource group is more valuable many times over than a representative sample"
>
> (Blumer 1969)

Group interviews will be used in this study as the only source of information due to their potential to provide detailed insight from teaching assistants perspectives about their own training and professional development. The validity of this approach can be supported by the views of Frey and Fontana (1993) who suggest that this is a distinct methodological justification for deploying group interviews in phenomenological research.

When selecting a participants for the research study it is important to consider how representative the sample will be of the whole population of teaching assistants in secondary schools in Surrey. Due to the time consuming nature of collecting data from group interviews and the restraints on the size of group to ensure manageability, it will not be possible to interview the entire population of teaching assistants at each school. Therefore a sample must be selected. It is important to try to ensure that the sample is free from bias.

"Sample needs to relate in some systematic manner to the social worlds and phenomena that a study seeks to throw light upon"

(King and Horrocks 2010p28)

To maintain the validity of the research the sample must fit with the other components of the study. Qualitative research will often use 'purposive sampling.' This is deliberate sampling with some purpose or focus in mind in which the researcher will select what she thinks is a typical sample (Punch 2009 and Walliman and Buckler 2008). Wolcott (1994) maintains that a large sample in qualitative research may lack the richness and depth of smaller studies. To gain meaningful data for this study the group must have experienced working with secondary school students with SEN. Therefore this sample will be small, consisting of three homogenous groups one from each secondary school. Each group will consist of four teaching assistants (1 HLTA and 3 TA) who have been working in secondary school for a minimum of 6 months, have experience of supporting SEN students in an inclusive classroom setting and are willing to take part in the study.

Methods of data analysis

Holliday (2002) describe data analysis as the processing of data, achieved by sifting, organising and cataloguing the information, then selecting and determining themes in order to make sense of the data. Punch (2009) expands further suggesting that qualitative data analysis methods depend on the purpose of the research and need to be systematic, disciplined, transparent and described to allow them to be scrutinized ensuring confidence in the findings. It is not the duty of the reader to make sense of the raw data. Data analysis allows the researcher to shift from making sense of what is encountered in the field, to making sense of the total experience to the reader. (Walliman and Buckler 2008, Holliday 2002).

The group interviews will be recorded and then transcribed verbatim by the researcher with simple additional notation where paralinguistic features clearly impact on meaning. It is important to use a consistent transcription style. Numerous authors have offered transcription systems, some highly complex such as Jefferson (1984) and others such as Silvermans (1993) being more concise. However, there are similarities in that they seek to capture aspects of speech that may impact on meaning. King and Horrocks (2010p145) have compiled a basic transcription system based primarily on Poland (2002) as well as others, it is this method of transcription that will be used in this study. Additional handwritten notes taken during the interview will detail any relevant non-verbal communication.

Walliman and Buckler (2008) suggest compiling a set of codes based on the background research to label different aspects of the study prior to conducting fieldwork. This is consistent with Coles and McGrath (2010) who suggest that data should be analysed using themes explored in the literature review to explain, explore and challenge. For this study themes in line with those identified during the literature review will be used as a guideline to ensure that the study remains relevant to the research question, however these will be refined if necessary during data collection and analysis.

Analysis will be conducted on each interview as soon as possible in the form of an initial interim analysis. Full analysis will not be carried out until all the data has been collected ensuring that issues and themes identified on the first analysis do not dominate those identified during subsequent transcripts, and in doing so potentially risk new issues and themes being overlooked. Data will be analysed by initially coding the data to identify who said what, on which line or page of the transcript that they said it, the theme it refers to and the particular issue within that theme that it relates to. This information will then be sorted into groups. The themes and issues will then be used to present the information logically whilst linking with other relevant themes and issues from the field study and data gathered during the literature review (Coles and McGrath 2010).

Ethical considerations

The ethical principle governing educational research is that participants should, not be harmed as a result of the study, be able to give their informed consent and receive anonymity. In addition the researcher must abide by all legal requirements including data protection. (BERA 2011).

"aim of the guidelines is to enable educational researchers to weigh up all aspects of the process of conducting educational research within any given context (from student research projects to large-scale funded projects) and to reach an ethically acceptable position in which their actions are considered justifiable"

(BERA 2011)

The nature and purpose of the research will be explained to the participants before asking if they are willing to be involved. On agreement, written explanation will be provided detailing the nature of the research and the option to withdraw at any stage. The participants will be assured anonymity, maintained by using pseudonyms to protect identity and confidentiality maintained by safeguarding and subsequently disposing the data collected. Written consent will be obtained. Participants will then be contacted to confirm a group interview date, time and venue. (Coles and McGrath 2010).

References

Balshaw M and Farrell P (2002) *Teaching Assistants* London: David Fulton Publishers Ltd

Blatchford P, Bassett P, Brown P, Martin C, Russell A and Webster R (2009) *Deployment and Impact of Support Staff Project* Institute of Education: University of London

Blumer H (1969) *Symbolic Interactionism: Perspective and Method* Berkeley CA University of California Press

Coles A and McGrath J (2010) *Your Education Research Project Handbook* Essex : Pearson Education Ltd

Dawson, Catherine. 2007., *Practical Guide to Research Methods, A: A User-Friendly Manual for Mastering Research Techniques and Projects. [online].* HowtoBooks. Available from:<http://www.myilibrary.com?ID=125396> 28 October 2013

Denscombe, Martyn. 2010., *Good Research Guide: For Small-Scale Social Research Projects, The : for small-scale social research projects. [online].* OpenUniversityPress. Available from:<http://www.myilibrary.com?ID=334359> 25 October 2013

DfES (1999) *The National Curriculum for England and Wales.* London: DfES.

Fontana A and Frey JH (1993) *The group interview in social research* in D L Morgan (ed) *Successful Focus Groups* London : Sage

Fontana A and Frey J H (1994) *Interviewing : the art of science* in Denkin N K and Lincoln Y S (eds) *Handbook of Qualitative Research*. Thousand Oaks CA : Sage (361-376)

HMI (2002) Teaching Assistants in primary schools: Evaluation

Holliday A (2002) Doing and Writing Qualitative Research London : Sage Publications Ltd

Jefferson G (1984) *Transcription Notation* in J Atkinson and J Heritage (eds) *Structures of Social Interaction* New York : Cambridge University Press

King N and Horrocks C (2010) *Interviews in Qualitative Research* London: Sage

Lincoln Y and Guba E (1985) Naturalistic Enquiry. Sage CA

Poland B D (2002) *Transcription Quality* in Gubrium JF and Holstein (eds) *Handbook of interview Research : Context and Method* Thousand Oaks CA : Sage

Punch K F (2009) *Introduction to Research Methods in Education.* London: Sage Publications Ltd

Roffey-Barentsen J (2012) *Voices from the Classroom : Perceptions and experiences of teaching assistants in primary, secondary and special schools* Saarbruken, Germany : Lambert Academic Publishing

Seale C Gobo G and Gubrium (1999) *The Quality of Qualitative Research* London : Sage

Silverman D (1993) *Interpreting Qualitative Data: Methods for Analysing Talk, Text and Interaction* London : Sage

Teeman D, Mundy E, Walker M, Scott E, Lin Y and Gallacher S (2009) *The support staff study: exploring experiences of training and development.* Available online at www.tda.gov.uk

Walliman N and Buckler S (2010) *Your dissertation in Education* London: Sage Publications Ltd

Wolcott H F (1994) *Transforming qualitative data: Descriptive Analysis and Interpretation.* Thousand Oaks : Sage

3. GINA BROWN

I am a Lead Learning Support Assistant in a secondary school in Surrey. I work with students from 11-16 across the curriculum although I mainly work in maths, which I love! I believe that completing the degree has enabled me to gain a much deeper level of knowledge in all aspects of Learning Support and has helped me to become much more effective in my role.

Title

An Exploration into teachers' perceptions of the effectiveness of Learning Support Assistants, in a mainstream secondary school in Surrey

Introduction

The purpose of the research project is to understand the perceptions of teachers regarding the effectiveness of Learning Support Assistants (LSAs). The study will make comparisons with recent research as well as with the views of a Teaching and Learning consultant who has been working with the school. The outcome of the study will be a detailed view of LSA deployment and practice from the point of view of the teachers and may lead to some recommendations for future deployment and practice of LSAs.

Rationale

The number of Support Staff within schools nationally has grown from 134,000 in 1997 to 346,000 in 2009 (Department of Education (DfE), 2010, p.7). The most significant increase has been in classroom based staff; reaching 181,600 in 2009 (DfE, 2010, p.7). For the purpose of this study classroom based staff will be referred to as Learning Support Assistants (LSAs) . This is to maintain consistency with the terminology used within the school featured in the study.

Recent, large scale research has resulted in negative headlines including "Army of teaching assistants faces the axe..." (Stevens, 2013). The Deployment and Impact of Support Staff in Schools (DISS) research (Blatchford et al, 2009) highlighted issues regarding the deployment and practice of support staff, specifically LSAs. The findings highlighted a discrepancy between teachers' perceptions and actual outcomes (Blatchford, Webster, Russell, 2012). However the DISS research has created controversy in terms of its quantitative methodological approach (DfE, 2010). Despite the headlines, the associated report does acknowledge that LSAs are a valued part of the school community (Blatchford, Webster, Russell, 2012). It is within this context that the research project will investigate the effectiveness of LSAs.

Ary (2010, p.35) states "constructs are abstractions that cannot be observed". The term 'effective' is a construct meaning "successful in producing a result or effect". (The Chambers Dictionary, 2008, p.491). A key aim of this study is to identify what the term 'effective' means to individual teachers and to use this as a basis for comparison between participants and literature. If teachers share an agreed idea of what constitutes effective use of LSAs it should be relatively straightforward to identify elements of good practice and areas for improvement. However if teachers have very different ideas on that central question, it may highlight a possible issue in terms of clarity of roles and expectations which are likely to limit the teachers' ability to use LSAs effectively.

Context

The research will be carried out at a mainstream secondary school in Surrey, where the researcher works as a Lead LSA. LSAs are based within the Learning Support Department and provide support to students on the Code of Practice in mainstream lessons. There are two Lead LSAs who have additional responsibilities. Both Lead LSAs have Higher Level Teaching Assistant (HLTA) status although the school does not utilise them as such. They perform the same role within the classroom as LSAs. There are five Learning Support teachers based within the Learning Support department who provide specialist literacy and numeracy lessons.

Research Question

The purpose of the study has defined the research question:

What are teachers' perceptions of the effectiveness of Learning Support Assistants in a mainstream secondary school in Surrey?

Literature Review

The Literature review will focus on key research regarding deployment and practice of LSAs. The DISS study forms the basis of reports by Blatchford, Russell and Webster (2012) and the DfE (2010) and is also the source of the headlines in national newspapers and is therefore central to the literature review. It will be discussed along with newspaper articles, Government documentation and other texts focusing on the role of LSAs.

The themes that have been identified are: reasons for the increase in support staff, background to recent headlines regarding the impact of LSAs; the professional status of LSAs and the effective deployment and practice of LSAs.

Methodology

"All forms of research are informed by underlying theoretical perspectives" (Wilson, 2013, p.18). According to Thomas (2013) ontology is concerned with understanding that there are different ways of viewing the world, based on assumptions about what exists in reality. In terms of research, Wilson (2013) affirms that ontology looks at what is being asked, in this case the effectiveness of LSAs. Thomas (2013) adds that epistemology is then concerned with how the question is studied or measured, in this case from the teachers' perspective.

Ary (2010, p.22) asserts that qualitative research "focuses on understanding social phenomena from the perspective of the human participants in natural settings". Given that the research question is specifically concerned with teachers' perceptions, this study clearly needs to have a qualitative approach. Andrews (2003) concurs, suggesting research questions that are concerned with attitudes will use a range of qualitative methods.

Newby (2010, p.44) defines a paradigm as "a set of rules that determine your research procedures". Thomas (2013, p.120) states "it is different ontological positions which lead on to the different paradigmatic positions." The subjective ontological and epistemological assumptions relating to the research question lead to the adoption of an interpretivist paradigm. Kidd, Abbott and Czerniawski (2003, p.92) aver interpretivists see the social world as "the sum of interactions between those who make up society". Ary (2010) suggests that an interpretative study attempts to understand phenomena through interpretation of participants' experiences. According to Thomas (2013) interpretivism begins with the assumption that the research cannot be completely objective. He goes on to emphasise the need for the researcher to recognise their own position so that they can minimise any risk of bias. The fact that the researcher is an LSA means that she will constantly need to be aware of her own position while conducting the research, using methods such as peer-validation to guard against bias.

The interpretivist paradigm allows for a range of methodologies. According to Ary (2010) a case study methodology focuses on a single unit and the research attempts to describe and understand that particular case. Bell (2010) suggests that it allows the researcher to look deeply at one issue as it is bound by specific parameters. The research question fits the case study methodology as it is focused on a single organisation. Bell (2010) claims the case study looks at how features and processes impact on the way that an organisation operates. This is concordant with the aims of this research project.

Data Collection

Newby (2010) asserts that methods of data collection must be robust and appropriate. In order to answer the research question, the perspectives of the teachers must be sought. The data will be gathered in the form of a qualitative questionnaire, featuring open questions. Ary (2010, p.423) states that qualitative research "typically use purposive sampling". The questionnaire will be sent to all teachers within the organisation, apart from the Learning Support teachers as they have a different role and do not teach mainstream classes. Interviews were considered as a tool for collection, however Thomas (2013) raises concerns that if the researcher is an insider within the organisation, participants may react differently. Similarly the British Educational Research Association (BERA) guidelines (2011, p.5) urge researchers to consider the impact on others, of fulfilling a dual role. In other words, participants may not real comfortable being interviewed by a colleague as it may affect their responses. Cohen, Manion and Morrison (2011) suggest participants tend to be more honest when answering questionnaires, due to their anonymity. Walliman and Buckler (2008) declare the need for clear and unambiguous language to be used in the questionnaires as misunderstandings cannot be clarified. It is therefore important to pilot the questionnaire. Thomas (2013) warns of potentially low return rates. The researcher will email a reminder to the participants during the data collection process. This can be repeated if necessary.

Cohen, Manion and Morrison (2011) define methodological triangulation as using different methods of data collection. The views of a Teaching and Learning Consultant, who has been working with the school, will be sought, in order to provide a further comparison, on top of the literature review. This will be in the form of a semi-structured interview. According to O'Hara et al (2011, p.171) semi-structured interviews allow themes and ideas relating to the research question to be explored, with the opportunity to ask probing questions to garner more detail.

A framework of questions will be developed which are in line with the questions featured in the questionnaire in order to ensure that the interview remains valid and relevant. The interview will last for 30 minutes and will be recorded using an audio device.

Data Analysis

Ary (2010) asserts that human behaviour is governed by context and as such it is important to convey the reality as it is perceived by the participant. Understanding the participant's feelings and behaviour within a given context is described as "Thick description" (Geertz, 1975, cited by Thomas, 2013, p.109).

Cohen, Manion and Morrison (2011, p.407) describe the process of data reduction, where the large amounts of data collected are reduced into "a form suitable for analysis". Walliman and Buckler (2008) recommend a process of coding whereby the results are reduced into a table of keywords, within which a tally can be created. It is likely that the questionnaires will arrive over a period of time so the data will subjected to what Ary (2010, p.425) terms "inductive analysis". The data will be coded as it arrives so that the researcher is constantly interpreting and categorising. The transcript from the consultant interview will use the same coding system to enable comparison, although it will be highlighted to mark it as distinct from the teacher participants. The data will be reviewed and refined, resulting in what Walliman and Buckler (2008, p.224) describe as a "gradual growth in understanding".

Validity and Reliability

BERA (2011, p.9) states methods of research must be "fit for purpose" and as such there is a need to justify the validity, reliability and generalisability of the research design.

"The questions you design need to provide you with the information necessary to answer your research question" (O'Hara et al, 2011, p.191). Walliman and Buckler

(2008) concur, urging researchers to ensure that they ask the right questions. The questionnaire will be peer-validated and will be piloted by the Learning Support teachers who are familiar with the organisation and role of the mainstream teachers within the school and are therefore able to check for bias and misunderstandings. The framework of questions for the consultant interview will also be peer-validated and will be cross-referenced against the questionnaire to ensure validity and reliability.

Thomas (2013, p.110) emphasises the need to present fair and balanced data, stating that "research, in this respect, is different from campaigning". The data collected could evoke an emotive response from the researcher as it is investigating the effectiveness of her role within the organisation. BERA (2011) suggest that researchers must be wary of potential conflicts of interest and it is essential that the researcher remains as objective as possible. Peer and supervisor validation will be used to check that the analysis remains balanced and fair.

Cohen, Manion and Morrison (2011) refer to external validity which is the extent to which research can be generalised across other communities or organisations. Thomas (2013) warns of the difficulties of generalising within social sciences and suggests that it is irrelevant in terms of case studies as they are concerned with one particular setting so it would be inappropriate to try to generalise from them. This research is a case study and as such is not generalisable.

Walliman and Buckler (2008, p.207) state "reliability refers to the consistency of the data", meaning the ability to replicate the results. They aver that if the questions that are asked are clear and unambiguous the data will be reliable. To that extent the peer-validation and piloting of the questionnaire should maximise the reliability.

Thomas (2013) advises researchers not to be overly concerned with reliability within the social sciences as it is of limited relevance although he does recommend the use of triangulation as a means of "seeing things from different angles" (2013, p.111). The consultant interview provides a second method to corroborate the teacher questionnaires; this provides methodological triangulation. In addition, the sample size means that participant triangulation can take place; also increasing reliability.

Ethical Considerations

Thomas (2013) asserts that ethics are concerned with how the researcher approaches the project in terms of conduct and respect for others. The research study will be conducted according to the ethical guidelines published by BERA (2011).

BERA (2011, p.5) advocate voluntary informed consent whereby "participants understand and agree to their participation, without any duress, prior to the research being undertaken". The teachers will be contacted via email which will contain the consent information. This will take the form of "implied consent" (Thomas, 2013, p.49) whereby the participants will be informed that it will be assumed that they agree to taking part in the research unless they specifically email the researcher to decline. This should maximise take up as well as maintaining the participants' anonymity.

BERA (2011) state the research needs to be confidential and anonymous and participants must be informed that they have the right to withdraw at any stage. The questionnaires will therefore be coded so that the researcher may identify and remove data should a participant withdraw. The data will be stored securely and the report will protect confidentiality and anonymity.

Wilson (2013) stresses the need to consider the effect that research may have on participants or anyone else affected by the results. The research focuses on the effectiveness of LSAs and therefore the results could affect the teachers and the Learning Support team. The research report will be made available for staff within the school to read. Wilson (2013) advocates using peer validation and advice, to ensure potentially unpopular messages are delivered in a way that will be seen as non-threatening. The report will not be advocating large scale changes. It will describe the current situation and may make some recommendations. The report will be peer-validated and advice will be sought from the study supervisor as well as the Head of Learning Support to ensure its objectivity and authenticity.

References

Andrews, R. (2003) *Research Questions*, London, New York: Continuum.

Ary, D., Jacobs, L.C. and Sorensen, C. (2010) *Introduction to Research in Education* (8th Edition), California: Wadsworth, Cengage Learning.

Bell. J. (2005) *Doing Your Research Project.* Maidenhead, Philadelphia: Open University Press. [Online] Available at: http://www.myilibrary.com?ID=94698 (Accessed 10 November 2013).

Blatchford, P., Bassett, P., Brown, P., Koutsoubou, M., Martin, C., Russell, A. and Webster, R., with Rubie-Davies, C. (2009) *Deployment and Impact of support staff in schools . The impact of support staff in schools. (Strand 2, Wave 2)* (DCF-RR1148). London: DfES. [Online]. Available at:

https://www.gov.uk/government/uploads/system/uploads/attachment_data/file/222049/DCSF-RR148.pdf (Accessed 23 November 2013).

Blatchford, P., Russell, A. and Webster, R. (2012) *Reassessing the Impact of Teaching Assistants*, Abingdon, New York: Routledge.

British Educational Research Association [BERA] (2011) *Ethical Guidelines for Educational Research 2011* [Online] Available at: http://www.bera.ac.uk/ (Accessed 25 November 2013).

The Chambers Dictionary (2008) *The Chambers Dictionary* (11th Edition), Edinburgh:

Chambers Harrap Publishers Ltd.

Cohen, L., Manion, L. and Morrison, K. (2011) *Research Methods in Education,* (7th Edition), Abingdon, New York: Routledge.

Department for Education [DfE] (2010) *School Support Staff Topic Paper* (DFE-RTP-10-001) [Online]. Available at:

https://www.gov.uk/government/uploads/system/uploads/attachment_data/file/183348/DFE-RTP-10-001.pdf (Accessed 23 November 2013).

Denscombe, M. (2010) *The Good Research Guide: For Small-Scale Social Research Projects.* Maidenhead, Philadelphia: Open University Press. [Online] Available at:http://www.myilibrary.com?ID=334359 (Accessed 10 November 2013).

Kidd, W., Abbott, D. and Czerniawski, G. (2003) *Sociology AS,* London: Heinemann

Newby, P. (2010) *Research Methods for Education*, Harlow: Pearson Education Limited.

O'Hara, M., Carter, C., Dewis, P., Kay, J. and Wainwright, J. (2011) *Successful Dissertations The Complete Guide for Education, Childhood and Early Childhood Studies Students,* London, New York: Continuum International Publishing Group.

Sikes, P., Nixon, J. and Carr, W. (2003) *The Moral Foundations of Educational Research: Knowledge, Inquiry and Values*, Maidenhead, Philadelphia: Open University Press.

Stevens. J. (2013) 'Army of Teaching assistants to be axed', *Mail Online*, 2 June [Online]. Available at: http://www.dailymail.co.uk/news/article-2334853/Army-teaching-assistants-faces-axe-Education-department-attempts-save-4billion-cost-year.html (Accessed 20 November 2013).

Thomas, G. (2013) *How to do your Research Project* (2nd Edition), London,

California, New Delhi, Singapore: SAGE Publications Ltd.

Walliman, N. and Buckler, S (2008) *Your Dissertation in Education*, London, California, New Delhi, Singapore: SAGE Publications Ltd.

Wilson, E. (2013) *School-based Research A guide for education students,* (2nd Edition), London, California, New Delhi, Singapore: SAGE Publications Ltd.

4. JULIA WHYBRA

I am a learning support assistant (LSA) and work at a large secondary school in North Hampshire. There are currently one thousand and fifty students on role. I support students within the classroom that have learning difficulties and behaviour issues. The majority of the classes that I work in are low ability. Within the classes that I support in, behaviour and concentration can be an issue. This is due to the learning difficulties that students have and behaviour issues such as Attention Deficit Hyperactivity Disorder (ADHD). Many students due to their behaviour issues and learning difficulties struggle to concentrate and understand what is being taught; therefore they will distract themselves or others in an attempt to avoid working. Within my role I will support students individually or in a small group. Maths is my subject so the majority of the lessons that I support in are maths lessons. Several times a week I withdraw students from maths lessons that have been identified by the teacher as needing extra support, and teach them individually or in a small group.

Title:

An Exploration of the Perceptions of Maths Homework for Year 10 Students.

Research Question:

In a North Hampshire secondary school, what is the Year 10 students' perspective on maths homework?

Aims:

This research project will investigate the perception of homework from the viewpoint of students in a year 10 maths class. The aim of the project is to assess the students' perception of maths homework, with regards to gaining an insight into the reasons as to why a number of students regularly fail to complete or even attempt the homework that is set for them. Areas for discussion will include; student ability, parental support and motivation. Following on from this, it will explore further the students' attitudes towards homework with a view to understanding and identifying how students can be supported and motivated to complete their homework.

Introduction

Teachers regularly setting work for students to complete at home has been common practice in many schools for some time. With maths in particular, it is a methodical subject and there can only be a right or wrong answer, there is no area that allows space for personal thoughts and opinions. Specific processes must be followed in order to answer questions, and the purpose behind the homework is for the student to practise what they have been taught in the lesson, which in turn should then reinforce the learning. This study is going to be focused on Year 10 students' perception of maths homework and will take place in a high achieving secondary school in North Hampshire that has a specialist status in mathematics and computing. The school celebrates outstanding General Certificate of Secondary Education (GCSE) results each year, in which the most recent results in 2013 saw eighty six per cent of students achieving five A* to C grades including Maths and English. Students are aware of the success of the school and are encouraged to embark on a positive, independent approach to their learning which is reflected in the school's motto 'Learning Without Limits'. Every student has four maths lessons a week and homework is set on a weekly basis. There is usually two parts to the homework that students need to complete; an online piece set on 'MyMaths' which is a subscription maths website where each student has their own unique log in and individual tasks, and a written piece relating to the current topic being studied, that is designed by the teacher. If students fail to complete the homework or hand it in on the due date, a detention will be given. The detention involves the student remaining at school after the close of the school day at three o'clock for a specific period of time. The detention will be with the student's maths teacher and the student will be expected to complete the homework during this time. This clearly impacts on a student's leisure time but despite this sanction being in place and consistently followed by the teachers, there are students who persistently fail to do their homework each week. The intention of this research project is to gather students' opinions on homework with a view to gaining an insight into the factors and outside influences that may affect and prevent students from completing their homework. Furthermore, an understanding of the students' perspective of maths homework will decide whether there is a need to review the current fashion in which homework is set, in order to fully support the students and their learning.

Proposed Literature

Punch (2008, p65) states that a proposal needs to "identify the body of literature which is relevant to the research, to indicate the relationship of the proposed study to the relevant literature". There has been an extensive amount of literature published on the topic of homework, however in order to stay relevant to the proposed research, the literature review will look at publications that in particular include students' opinions on homework. Furthermore, written works on student motivation in regards to homework will support the research genre. In addition, there have been recently published articles voicing the views of select groups of government officials, teachers and parents that have questioned whether homework is fit for its purpose. Barker (2013) when researching into the issues surrounding homework reported that "homework has remained a political and emotive issue for well over a century". Such literature will help give an overview of public opinion on homework, and help the researcher to identify if the opinion of the students reflects this or whether the students have a different perception of homework and its purpose.

Methodology

Ontology is the:

> Theory of being and existence, how you and other living things
> exist in the world and what you believe is out there.
>
> Wisker (2009, p60)

This research is based on human opinion and feelings so the ontology of this project will be subjective as it will presume that the truth is not scientific, but as a result of human nature and society itself. Epistemology is a:

> Philosophical concept concerning how you know what you know
> and the methods you use in order to test the validity of
> knowledge.
>
> Davies (2007, p236)

The epistemology of this research will assume that knowledge is interpretation and that meaning exists in our interpretations of the world. Therefore, on reflection of the ontological and epistemological assumptions, the approach to this research will be from an interpretivist paradigm. Arthur et al (2012, p16) state that "Interpretivism does not see direct knowledge as possible; it is the accounts and observations of the world that provide indirect indications of phenomena".

This project will be qualitative research and for this purpose will adopt a case study approach. A case study will allow the researcher to gather primary data directly from the students and compare to the findings in the literature review. Cohen, Manion and Morrisson (2011, p289) state that:

> A case study provides a unique example of real people in real
> situations, enabling readers to understand ideas more clearly
> than simply by presenting them with abstract theories or

principles.

The research is focused in particular on the views of Year 10 students. However, as there are nearly two hundred Year 10 students at the secondary school where the research will be based, a suitable sample of students will be selected in order to carry out the research.

Methods of Data Collection

Walliman (2011, p173) declares that:

> The reasons for choosing particular data collection and analysis
> methods are always determined by the nature of what you want
> to find out, the particular characteristics of your research
> problem and the specific sources of information.

The researcher will be collecting qualitative data as the research question is based upon the thoughts and opinions of year 10 students. Burton et al (2008, p146) advise that "qualitative evidence is most often associated with the interpretive paradigm".

The main focus of the research is to gather the opinions of the students. Therefore, in order to answer the research question effectively, the preferred method of data collection will be in the form of a semi structured interview. A semi structured interview is where the researcher will have a specific number of questions on the chosen topic, but has the freedom to elaborate and clarify the questions to the interviewee. The questions asked will mainly be open questions as the researcher is seeking the interviewee's opinion. Robson (2011, p285) expresses that a semi structured interview is:

> Most appropriate when the interviewer is closely involved with
> the research process (e.g. in a small – scale project when the

researcher is also the interviewer).

The interviews will be recorded using an audio recorder so as to ensure the researcher has an account of all of the students' responses given in the interviews. However, a disadvantage to recording interviews is that body language and facial expressions can obviously not be recorded, so therefore it is useful for the researcher to make notes on this during the interviews.

The research will take place within a year 10 maths class that the researcher supports in herself. The class is a small class with only ten students .Two of the students within the class have English as an additional language (EAL) and communication can at times be a barrier. As the aim of the research is to identify the reasons as to why some students regularly fail to complete their homework, the students that will be included in the interviews will be those identified by the teacher, that repeatedly do not do their homework. Each student will be asked exactly the same questions by the researcher in the same format. The interviews will take place during the students' maths lesson so will not cause disruption to their school day.

There is a danger of researcher bias with this chosen method as the researcher is well known to the students. The students may not answer the questions truthfully for fear of upsetting the researcher. There is a possibility that their responses to the questions asked, will only reflect what they feel the researcher wants to hear rather than their true feelings. In contrast, the researcher as she knows the students well could also interpret their answers according to what she believes their perception of homework to be.

Methods of Data Analysis

Bryman (2012, p13) explains that:

> The data analysis stage is fundamentally about data reduction –
> that is, it is concerned with reducing the large corpus of
> information that the researcher has gathered so that he or she
> can make sense of it.

The process of data analysis will commence during the data collection. In addition to the recordings of the interviews, the researcher will take notes of the non-verbal communication after each interview and produce a transcript to support the data analysis. Dawson (2012, p115) advises that to help with the analysis of qualitative data:

> It is useful to produce an interview summary form which you
> complete as soon as possible after each interview has taken
> place. This includes practical details about the time and place,
> the participants, the duration of the interview and details Of
> emerging themes.

After the interview process has been completed, the researcher will interpret the qualitative data that has been collected by using thematic analysis. Thematic data analysis involves grouping the data into themes or categories that are relevant to the research question. The researcher will look for patterns in the data and whether key words or terms are repeated throughout the interview process. Furthermore, the researcher will look to see whether any comparisons can be made between individual students' answers.

The researcher is conducting the research from an interpretative philosophy and is interested in the Year 10 perceptions of maths homework, their thoughts on the purpose of homework, and the reasons as to why they do not complete their homework. Once the data analysis is completed, the researcher will discuss her findings with the class teacher as the overall aim is to encourage and support the students to do their homework. Furthermore, the findings may have an influence on whether there is a need to change the way in which the maths homework is set.

Validity and Reliability

Davies (2007, p243) states that:

> In all types of research, the concept of validity relates to the question of whether the end results of your analysis are accurate representations of the psychosocial or textual reality that you claim them to be.

The data collection methods used will give the research validity as they allow the researcher to collect the participants' views in line with the research question. Furthermore, the data collected will be primary data. The researcher however needs to take care when analysing the data as they need to ensure that the collected data represents the participants' true feelings, and is not influenced by their own thoughts. Researcher bias may be an issue. Bryman (2012, p39) informs that:

> It is common, for researchers working within a qualitative research strategy, and in particular when they use participant observation or interviewing, to develop a close affinity with the people whom they study to the extent that they find it difficult to disentangle their stance as social scientists from their subjects' perspective.

In addition, the researcher needs to be aware with a focus group that group dynamics may play a part in influencing individual student's answers. The students' responses to the questions asked may not be their true beliefs but a reflection of what other group members have already expressed. Moreover, one student may dominate the group or be reluctant to speak in front of other group members (Cohen, Manion and Morrisson, 2011).

In order for research to be reliable, the process must be repeatable and achieve the same results regardless of the researcher. This research has an interpretivist approach. The data collected is based on people's thoughts and feelings, so therefore it is not possible for the researcher to make generalisations from the results of the research. This means that there are limitations to the reliability of the research, therefore it can make the research unreliable. However, in an effort to overcome this issue, the researcher will ensure the students in the focus group remain the same throughout the research and that each student is asked the same questions in the same setting. However, there is always a risk that the students would not give the same responses if interviewed by a different researcher.

Ethics

Prior to commencing this research, it is essential that the ethics of research are considered. According to Sharp (2012, p22) research carried out in an ethically proper manner:

> Ensures that all appropriate steps are taken to protect the interests, status, values and beliefs of all participants and organisations, including you from harm.

Throughout this research project, the researcher will comply with the ethical guidelines for research that have been established by the British Educational Research Association (BERA). Before the students partake in the project, the researcher must seek consent from the school, the students and their parents. The participants need to be informed of the researcher's intentions and in addition, what will become of the data that is collected. Researchers need to ensure that they do not manipulate the students in any manner. The students that will be involved in the research project will be the age of fourteen or fifteen and are considered to be young people rather than children. However, BERA (2011) require that researchers when working with young people also comply with articles three and twelve of the United Nations Convention on the Rights of the Child, and express that "the best interests of the child must be the primary consideration". Furthermore, "children who are capable of expressing their own views should be granted the right to express their views freely" and should therefore "be facilitated to give fully informed consent". Finally, it is the researcher's responsibility to make the students aware that they have the right to withdraw from the research project at any point and without reason.

References

Arthur, J., Waring, M., Coe, R and Hedges, L. (2012) *Research Methods and Methodologies in Education.* London: Sage Publications Ltd.

BERA (2011) 'Ethical Guidelines for Educational Research' [Online]. Available at: http://www.bera.ac.uk/publications/Ethical%20Guidelines. (Accesses 19th October 2013).

Bryman, A. (2012) 4th edn. *Social Research Methods.* Oxford: Oxford University Press.

Burton, N., Brundrett, M and Jones M. (2008) *Doing Your Education Research Project.* London: Sage Publications Ltd.

Barker, I. (2013) 'Is it time to scrap homework?' Times Educational Supplement [Online]. Available at: http://www.tes.co.uk/article.aspx?storycode=6319948. (Accessed 14th October 2013).

Cohen, L., Manion, L and Morrisson, K. (2011) 7th edn. *Research Methods in Education.* Oxon: Routledge.

Davies, M. (2007) *Doing a Successful Research Project Using Qualitative or Quantitative Methods.* Basingstoke: Palgrave Macmillan.

Dawson, C. (2012) *Introduction to Research Methods – A practical guide for anyone undertaking a research project.* Oxford: How to Books Ltd.

Punch, K. (2008) 2nd edn. *Developing Effective Research Proposals.* London: Sage Publications Ltd.

Robson, C. (2011) 3rd edn. *Real World Research.* Chichester : John Wiley and Sons Ltd.

Sharp, J. (2012) 2nd edn. *Success with your Education Research Project.* London: Learning Matters.

Walliman, N. (2011) 3rd edn. *Your Research Project.* London: Sage Publications Ltd.

Wisker, G. (2009) *The Undergraduate Research Book.* Basingstoke: Palgrave Macmillan.

5. LISA BLOGG

At the time of writing my BA (Hons) proposal for my dissertation, I worked as a teaching assistant in a Year 5 class in an outstanding rural primary school in the South of England. Having worked as a teaching assistant in various primary schools for over 12 years and in that particular primary school for over six years, I began to wonder whether the behaviour of pupils would be affected by the use of extrinsic motivational rewards, such as raffle tickets. In particular, my studies led me specifically towards the perceptions of the teachers who taught the Year 5 pupils and whether the teachers themselves thought that pupils responded positively towards the raffle tickets, which were awarded for good behaviour during lessons and around the school. The raffle tickets which had been awarded were placed in weekly Year 5 raffle ticket draws, with stationery items such as pens and pencils, awarded as prizes. Nationally at that time, Ofsted focussed upon pupil behaviour management as one of their key objectives in school inspections and so, upon reflection, the use of extrinsic motivational rewards and whether they would affect pupil behaviour presented itself as a topical and worthy focus for the proposal for my dissertation.

Currently, I am in the process of completing my BA (Hons) and have been offered a place on a teacher training course, after which, I hope to further my career and become a primary school teacher.

Title

A Case Study into whether an extrinsic motivational reward will affect behaviour in a Year Five class in a South of England Primary School.

Introduction

Rationale for carrying out the research

This case study will investigate whether extrinsic motivational rewards will affect pupil behaviour in a Year Five class in a South of England Primary School. The use of extrinsic rewards will be discussed, before focusing upon their motivational use in education and how they may affect pupil behaviour.

This study will be set in an average-sized rural primary school. The School Improvement Plan 2012/2014 (2012) identifies behaviour as a key issue and an area for development, whilst recommending staff actively reward positive behaviour. The school places a strong emphasis (School Behaviour Policy, 2009) upon reward systems to maintain high behavioural standards. Rewards range from whole-school house-points to individual pupil reward systems, reflecting the National Foundation for Educational Research (NFER) national survey findings that "82% of teachers" (NFER, 2012:1) employ reward systems. The Office for Standards in Education Framework for school inspection (Ofsted) (2013) also focuses upon pupil behaviour management as a key objective in schools.

The case study's focus derived from the researcher's interest regarding pupils' behaviour and extrinsic rewards. The results of this study will either reinforce the research question (behaviour is affected) or will not reinforce it (behaviour is not affected) (Cohen, Manion and Morrison, 2011). The following research question was formulated from the research title.

Research question

Will an extrinsic raffle ticket motivational reward affect pupil behaviour?

Proposed literature

Walliman (2011) identifies literature reviews as fundamental tasks relating to research projects, whilst Hart (1998) suggests, they confirm a project's researchability.

This literature review will discuss relevant literature and research regarding extrinsic motivational rewards and their educational application, plus children's extrinsic orientation. Selecting key words, Denscombe (2002) suggests, will enable this study to remain focused, identify key issues and appropriate data collection techniques (Hart, 2004) whilst assisting in analytical assessments of methodology design. Literature reviews are the beginning of the critical thinking stage, Bell (2010) suggests; where assumptions are queried, facts are classified and important claims are debated. Thus adopting a "critical and analytical manner" (Malthouse and Roffey-Barentsen, 2013:2).

Methodology

The study's ontology assumes that natural truth is socially constructed; allowing numerous subjective realities, including researchers, participants and audiences to exist (Creswell, 1998). The epistemology assumes close researcher-participant interaction, knowledge and interpretation of past experiences (Newby, 2010) will enable the study to "shape multiple beliefs and values" (Cohen, Manion and Morrison, 2011:33).

Interpretivism

This study aligns with the interpretivist paradigm, adopting an interpretivist approach, due to its ontological and epistemological assumptions. Interpretivists assume knowledge and theory emerge via individuals' interpretations of the world (Cohen, Manion and Morrison, 2011). Interpretivism works with the world, making sense of human perceptions (Scott and Usher, 2011), scaffolding pre-understandings through interpretive frameworks. However, the researcher is aware that their personal views, assumptions and direct involvement with the participants may influence the study, reflecting Hennink, Hutter and Bailey (2011), who suggest researchers should be mindful of imposing their personal influences during research.

In contrast, the positivist approach assumes "explanation proceeds by way of scientific description" (Cohen, Manion and Morrison, 2011:7). The positivist ontological and epistemological stance is objective, assuming that meaning and truth already exist in the world, regardless of the subjective interpretivism of individuals' perceptions (Bell, 2010). Positivist epistemology assumptions align with French philosopher Auguste Comte, who believed knowledge reflects reality, which is investigated through experimentation and observation (Newby, 2010), thereby producing observable and measurable quantitative research. Consequently, a positivistic approach was not selected for this study, due to the researcher's and study's alignment with interpretivist assumptions.

Case study approach

A case study approach was selected to conduct this small-scale research project because it will focus upon the teacher's views and interpretations regarding extrinsic raffle ticket rewards affecting pupil's behaviour. Case study approaches enable detailed, in-depth analysis of specific events (Newby, 2010), which are "bounded by time and place" (Creswell, 1998:37). Bell (2010) also advocates case study approaches, suggesting them as ideal methodologies, which demonstrate the functionality of specific systems, such as raffle ticket reward systems. However, Newby (2010) implies case studies can lead researchers to inaccurate conclusions. Consequently, the researcher will remain reflective, impartial and focused upon the project's aim.

Methods of data collection

Although Bell (2010) suggests not one data collection method can be discounted when applying case study approaches, interviews and observations are commonly employed. However, this study will use a semi-structured questionnaire to systematically collect qualitative data within restrictive time constraints, due to its structured layout (Newby, 2010). The researcher acknowledges all methods have their advantages and disadvantages (Bell, 2010) and will endeavour to reduce them, by for example, using detailed questioning.

Semi-structured questionnaire

Traditionally questionnaires are viewed as quantitative, producing large amounts of numerical data (Newby, 2010). Nevertheless it was felt that a qualitative semi-structured questionnaire would be most suitable, as it would minimise the impact upon the teaching commitments of participating staff, whilst maintaining maximum pupil learning time (Hopkins 2002).

Koshy (2010) suggests questionnaires can be viewed as quick methods of gathering suitably detailed data. However, Newby (2010) implies questionnaires can be problematic; displaying disadvantages including difficult analytical challenges, besides initiating bias. Nevertheless, it was decided that questionnaires would be most suitable, due to the study's small scale and time restrictions as opposed to interviews or observations, because the latter would need pre-arranging with participants at mutually convenient times, besides raising additional ethical considerations. Focus groups were also dismissed, due to participants possibly electing to withhold their views in front of others.

Bell (2010) suggests data collection methods should be chosen due to their suitability in response to research questions, paradigms and time constraints, as opposed to their alignment with traditional beliefs. Koshy (2010) agrees suggesting carefully chosen data collection methods producing quality data are vitally important in ensuring successful research conclusions.

Initially, a pilot group will be invited to complete pilot questionnaires, enabling the researcher to ascertain if proposed questions will produce appropriate qualitative data to answer the research question. This reflects the beliefs of Cohen, Manion and Morrison (2011), which imply piloting chosen data collection methods highlight potential weaknesses, safeguard against question ambiguity and identify technical problems. Newby (2010) warns against the careless phrasing of questions, which could generate unwanted superfluous data. Ambiguous questions can then be rectified before the final questionnaire is distributed.

Six teachers will be invited to complete semi-structured questionnaires over a six week period. The teachers were selected because they are all familiar with the pupils and currently teach (or have taught) the class during this term, because the class teacher is newly qualified and so entitled to additional planning and preparation time.

Questionnaires will be sealed in envelopes, along with return envelopes for completed questionnaires, and will conclude with directions of where they can be anonymously and securely left for the researcher to collect. Questionnaires will be given out to teachers on a one-to-one basis by the researcher and will be numbered from one to six, reflecting Creswell's (1998) suggestions of continual participant anonymity. Participants will be asked to date their questionnaire as this will assist in the cross-correlation with raffle tickets. The questionnaire will contain a selection of closed, multiple-choice and open questions, which will lead teachers through the questionnaire process (Bell, 2010), enabling teachers to voice their views.

Methods of data analysis

Qualitative data produced by questionnaires will be collated, scrutinized, interpreted and analysed question by question. Commonality will be looked for between data, including word patterns, frequencies, themes and emerging ideas (Creswell, 1998). However, Bell (2010) warns that questionnaire data may be of little value to the study, until analysed, interpreted and evaluated. Consequently, the researcher will guard against misinterpreting participants' answers, until the data analysis process is complete, in case unexpected results and anomalies are discovered (Mason, 2002). However, by grouping and coding any recurring themes, it is envisaged that any anomalies will be identified and discussed accordingly.

The raffle tickets allocated during the study will be collected; acting as secondary data. The qualitative data produced by the questionnaires will be compared to the secondary data, highlighting otherwise invisible themes or patterns, which may have remained undetected. Wilson and Fox (2009) cited in Wilson (2013) advocate using multiple sources of data collection, suggesting they nurture researcher's emerging knowledge of developing situations.

Data analysis results will be appropriately communicated to readers (Bell, 2010), for example by creating tables, as (Creswell, 1998) suggests these are immediate ways of displaying comparisons.

Validity and Reliability

To ensure validity, this study will have clear correlations between qualitative data collected and the research question. Precise questions will obtain qualitative primary data, with secondary data enhancing the study's validity, so providing triangulation (Newby, 2010).

Qualitative research, involving people's interpretations of the world (Bell, 2010), can by its very nature, Creswell (1998) suggests, be valid yet unreliable. This study will attempt to limit unreliability by incorporating secondary data, as Newby (2010) recommends, through cross-comparison of primary and secondary data which supports and strengthens reliability and validity.

However, to be deemed reliable, Bell (2010) suggests, research must be replicable and repeatable. Other researchers should be able to perform exactly the same research under the same conditions, generating the same results and not simply a one-off. Consequently, as raffle tickets (only displaying dates and subjects) are awarded to pupils at various times throughout the school day by different teachers, exactly the same conditions would not be replicable (Cohen, Manion and Morrison, 2011). Identical results would probably not be obtained because other researchers would not be familiar with the teachers, pupils or the setting. The similarity of other studies against this study (Bell, 2010) will determine how relatable this study becomes, so affecting its generalisability.

This study will use a sample of six teachers, all of whom know the researcher and so the researcher may unwittingly introduce bias, which will affect the study's reliability and validity. Continuous reflection upon this will allow the researcher to contain any personal or subjective influences throughout the study. Further validity will be sought by piloting the questionnaire, enabling potential questioning ambiguities to be addressed and so ensuring all participants will be asked identical questions.

Ethics

This study will adhere to BERA (British Ethical Research Association) (2011) ethical guidelines by maintaining participant's anonymity (BERA, 2011), which Creswell (1998) suggests, can be further protected by assigning numbers to participant's questionnaires, which will be replicated within this study.

Prior to the study commencing, overall consent will be obtained from the headteacher (gatekeeper). Bell (2010) suggests, as the study will occur within normal day-to-day school routines and not involve the pupils directly, pupil-parent consent will not be required (Newby, 2010), as the headteacher's overall consent will be adequate (BERA, 2011).

Additionally, as the researcher has a close involvement with the teachers, the use of observations and interviews was dismissed because it was felt that the researcher's presence within the classroom could affect the pupil's and teacher's behaviours, which is known as the Hawthorne effect (Cohen, Manion and Morrison, 2011). Consequently, to ensure that pupils will not behave differently during the study, allowing appropriate data to be obtained, Bell (2010) suggests pupils need not be informed that the study is occurring, aligning with BERA (2011) guidelines. The headteacher is aware and fully supports this decision.

It was felt that the ethical implications of questionnaires would be most appropriate at protecting participants' anonymity. Questionnaires will inform participants of the study's aim, requirements, data usage, rights to comment upon the results and receive feedback upon completion (Newby, 2010). Participants will be notified of their rights to anonymity, nonparticipation (Nuremberg Code, 1949) and withdrawal from the study at any given time (Greig and Taylor, 1999). The researcher will ensure that participants are fully informed and willing (BERA, 2011), before the study commences so ensuring voluntary informed consent is achieved. Questionnaires will adhere to "minimal intrusion" (Scottish Educational Research Association, 2013:5) ethical requirements, asking only relevant questions related to the study's aim, whilst containing no-opinion options, enabling participants to withhold their views (Newby, 2010).

Data will be collected and securely stored in locked cupboards. Once completed and submitted in June 2013, the ethical implications determine all study data and documents will be destroyed (BERA, 2011).

References

Bell, J. (2010) *Doing Your Research Project,* 5th ed, Maidenhead: Open University Press

British Educational Research Association (2011) *Ethical Guidelines for Educational Research,* London: BERA [online]. Available from: http://www.bera.ac.uk/publications/Ethical%20Guidelines [Accessed 11th November 2013]

Cohen, L., Manion, L. and Morrison, K. (2011) *Research Methods in Education,* 7th ed, Oxon: Routledge

Creswell, J. W. (1998) *Qualitative Inquiry and Research Design: choosing among five traditions,* London: Sage

Denscombe, M. (2002) *Ground Rules for Good Research: A 10 point guide for social researchers,* Maidenhead: University Press

Greig, A. and Taylor, J. (1999) *Doing Research with Children,* London: Sage

Hart, C. (1998) *Doing a Literature Review,* London: Sage

Hennink, M., Hutter, I. and Bailey, A. (2011) *Qualitative Research Methods,* London: Sage

Hopkins, D. (2002) *A Teachers Guide to Classroom Research,* Maidenhead: Open University

Koshy, V. (2010) *Action Research,* 2nd ed, London: Sage

Malthouse, R. and Roffey-Barentsen, J. (2013) *Research Projects and Dissertations,* London: Thalassa Publishing

Mason, J. (2002) *Qualitative Researching,* London: Sage

Newby, P. (2010) *Research Methods for education,* Harlow: Pearson Education Limited

National Foundation for Educational Research (2012) *NFER Teacher Voice Omnibus February 2012 Survey: pupil behaviour* (DFE Research Report 219), London: DFE [online]. Available from:
http://www.nfer.ac.uk/nfer/publications/91054/91054_home.cfm?publicationID=703&title=NFER%20Teacher%20Voice%20Omnibus%20February%202012%20survey (Accessed 30th October 2013)

School, (2009) Behaviour Policy

School, (2012) School Improvement Plan 2012/2014

Scott, D. and Usher, R. (2011) *Researching Education: Data, Methods and Theory in Educational Enquiry,* 2nd ed, London: Continuum

Scottish Educational Research Association (2005) Ethical Guidelines for Educational Research, Edinburgh: SERA [online]. Available from:
http://www.sera.ac.uk/documents/Publications/SERA%20Ethical%20GuidelinesWeb.PDF (Accessed 3rd November 2013)

The Nuremberg Code (1949) [online]. Available from:
http://www.sciencemuseum.org.uk/broughttolife/techniques/nurembergcode.aspx (Accessed 2nd November 2013)

The Office for Standards in Education (Ofsted). The Framework for School Inspection (2013), Manchester: Ofsted [online]. Available from:
http://webarchive.nationalarchives.gov.uk/20110809101133/ofsted.gov.uk/resources/framework-for-inspection-of-maintained-schools-england-september-2009

(Accessed 1st November 2013)

Walliman, N. (2011) *Your Research Project: designing and planning your work,* 3rd ed, London: Sage

Wilson, E. and Fox, A. (2009) 'Collecting Data', in E. Wilson (Ed) *School-based research: A guide for education students,* 2nd ed, London: Sage Publications, pp 103-124

6. MONICA LOCK

I am currently working as a childminder, where I have complete responsibility for all aspects of working with young children in my care. This includes being the Key Person, Child Protection Officer, accountant, chief cook and bottle washer!

I began my career in accounts but after having my children Robert and Tom, it became clear I should pursue a more fulfilling role in caring or teaching and moved into fostering. From there I went on to complete my Foundation Degree and am currently studying for my BA (Hons) in education.

I hope this will open up other opportunities for me and aim to become a College lecturer. Studying for the BA has shown me I have a love for research and a determination and dedication I never realised. I recommend Further Education to everybody

Title

Risk Taking – Good or Bad?

Introduction

When taking a risk we make a judgement on what the probability of something occurring is, and if it does happen, how it will affect us (Gladwin and Collins, 2008). Practitioners working within the Early Years make constant assessments of risk on behalf of young children. The judgements they make will be dictated firstly by the setting's policies but also from personal, highly subjective, perspectives.

Literature appears to indicate that Early Years practitioners should allow children to take reasonable risks within their play to learn and hone life skills, and build the self-esteem which comes with these skills. Gill (2007:16) states "overcoming challenging situations is an essential part of living a meaningful and satisfying life." Yet in reality there seems to be a reluctance for practitioners to do this. Childminders, in particular, work on their own and responsibility is all on their shoulders as: there is no collaboration on a daily or hourly basis, there is no one to watch their backs, they write their own policies, and ultimately, the buck stops with them. Therefore personal judgement and risk assessment are of great significance to a child's safety and general well-being.

Taking a risk comes in many forms from having the emotional confidence to try something new, to failing and having the confidence to try again, to meeting the physical challenges in life such as learning how to swim. With the development of confidence and self-esteem being so important Vygotsky's and Bruner's theory of scaffolding (Miller, 2002) seems most pertinent here. This is where a child attempting a new challenge is shown at first by the adult under close supervision. For example, when teaching a child to ride a bicycle, the adult will firmly hold the handlebar and seat around the child reassuring them of their safety. Gradually the scaffolding is removed at the appropriate rate as the child gains confidence and skill in the task. In the case of the bicycle the adult lets go of the seat, then the handlebar and eventually stops running alongside the child and watches them cycle alone, having mastered the task. The scaffolding can be put back a step at any stage depending on the child's needs and level of confidence and capability.

This being the case one could question how a childminder becomes competent in making judgements as to the risk involved in everyday activities which they undertake with their charges. No specific training or guidance, focussed on what is considered 'acceptable risk', is available through either the Professional Association for Childcare and Early Years (PACEY) or local authorities on behalf of

Ofsted. Therefore childminders have no fixed criteria by which to measure how far they should allow children to go in any potentially risky situation.

Before proposing that training, or guidance, is required for childminders in the area of assessing risk, a baseline of current knowledge and level of practice of childminders must be determined. This will be determined through asking a sample of childminders the following questions:

1. How much risk do they allow a child to take in different situations?
2. What was the reasoning behind those decisions?
3. Have childminders received any training on risk taking?
4. If specific training were offered, what would childminders gain from it?

The outcome of the research will indicate if training would be beneficial to childminder's decisions regarding risk taking. Naturally this will only prove of benefit if, as promoted by John Furlong (James, 2012:182), "knowledge transfer" takes place by "working directly with professionals", i.e. gaps in knowledge are filled through development of a training programme.

Research Question

Are childminders provided with sufficient training and guidance to enable them to support children in taking acceptable risks or are they reliant on personal attitudes, developed through their own experiences, and would specific training provide an alternative view?

Proposed Literature

The literature review will seek to find guidance through a broad spectrum of reading (Malthouse and Roffey-Barentsen, 2013) on risk taking in Early Years. The purpose of the literature review is to familiarise myself with the subject, gaining a background including others work upon the subject, and contrasting opinions

(Sharp, 2009). This begins with general text such as Gill (2007) showing the importance of taking appropriate risks.

Howard et al (2002) will be looked at to link the importance of experiences to assessments. These journals provide cutting edge views with the most recent thinking as to what is important and the true outcome of the research, without (significant) influence from the author. Wider reading of journal papers will enable me to start forming an opinion as to what is important for my specific topic.

The review proposes to examine Ofsted's guidance and statutory requirements as they are the governing body for Early Years Workers. In particular it will look at The Early Years Foundation Stage (DFE, 2012) views on risk assessment and policies.

The question of what childminders actually have to fear if a child is injured whilst in their care, provided they have not been negligent, must be reflected upon, with legislative Acts such as The Children Act 2004 (TSO, 2004) being considered. In the same vein, guidelines from Health and Safety Executive (HSE, 2012) shall be researched.

Methodology

Effective research follows set steps in a systematic way to draw conclusions on a subject using one of several approaches. This project will adopt an epistemological approach as it questions childminder's concepts on the subject and their actual practices in reality. (Cohen *et al,* 2011)

As this whole subject depends on human judgement, based on practitioner's experiences, assessment of risk in Early Years must take a subjective philosophical stance, using an interpretivist research paradigm. "The interpretive paradigm … is characterised by a concern for the individual… To understand the subjective world of human experience." (Cohen *et al*, 2007:21). This is opposed to the positivists view, where the world must be watched and measureable (Walliman and Buckler,

2008).

The research will be carried out on childminders, within two childminding groups with approximately fifteen members each, in a relatively affluent urban area of South-East England, being predominantly white British.

Due to the nature of their child-centred, self-employed work childminders are difficult to pin down for study. Therefore a survey will be used.

> Investigators administer a survey to a sample or to the entire population of people to describe the attitudes, opinions, behaviours, or characteristics of the population. In this procedure, survey researchers collect quantitative, numbered data using questionnaires … and statistically analyze the data to describe trends about responses to questions and to test research questions or hypotheses.

> (Creswell, 2013:402)

Being a questionnaire, the childminders will be fully aware of their consensual participation and therefore the process will be overt.

A questionnaire will be designed to determine individual childminder's approaches to various scenarios or aspects regarding children's everyday risk taking. The Likert Scale will be used as it is "… successfully used to measure people's attitudes" (Roberts-Holmes, 2011:174), which is most pertinent to this research question. The questionnaires will be given out at the childminding groups, any members who are absent on the day will receive them in the post. Consent forms will be given or sent with the questionnaire.

As cautioned by Bell (2010), whilst designing and using a questionnaire care must be taken to avoid the common pitfalls such as ambiguous wording, causing offence and two questions in one. Questionnaires are limited in the data gained with predetermined answers. However, in this case, it is a semi-structured questionnaire where opinions are also being sought for further clarification. Although difficult to design, some of the advantages of questionnaires are: a quick method of gaining information, respondent's anonymity, lack of interviewers prejudice and ease of data analysis (Gillham, 2007).

Data collection

Questionnaires using the Likert scale method will be sent to approximately 30 childminders, gaining results of a numerical nature. Different scenarios will be presented as statements. There will only be 4 possible answers in each case, ranging from "strongly agree" to "strongly disagree", to eliminate the chance of all replies falling into the "not sure" area as this would make results inconclusive.

 Although the questionnaire will be using the Likert scale, it will be adapted to incorporate free text questions for childminders to give further information regarding opinions and attitudes. This will give results of a narrative nature as it will be gathering people's opinions. This adaption has been chosen as it was originally hoped to gather information from a questionnaire, followed by a focus group to gather further information. However, due to practical issues such as time, venue, et cetera this will not be possible. By adding the free text questions it is hoped to gather similar information. Therefore the questionnaire will be made of both closed questions, with fixed answers, and open questions in the free text boxes where a participant will write their own answer. There will also be a small section of questions to gain personal data such as 'how long have you been a childminder?' Gillham (2007) describes these as subject descriptors which will add depth to the overall picture.

A pilot questionnaire will be used on two or three childminders to check for flaws in its design.

Data Analysis

Bell (2010) recommends that before analysis begins, data should be checked for manageability and relevance to the research question.

The Likert scale method will give numerical, quantitative data from the closed questions. This can be collated relatively easily, displaying the results in charts or graphs the easily recognisable levels of risk childminders are prepared to let children take (Gillham, 2007).

The more open 'free text' questions will give qualitative data, with opinions being interpreted in a more narrative way. This will generate more data and analysis must focus on the research question, staying true to research values. The conclusion must be drawn from evidence, following a systematic approach, rather than loosely interpreted findings (Smith *et al*, 2009).The analysis will look for common phrases, themes, patterns et cetera. Because of the larger amount of data, Silverman (2005) recommends starting analysis of qualitative nature as it arrives, not waiting until it is all together.

Quantitative and qualitative data can then be cross-referenced to check the reliability and validity of both sets of data as it will provide more than one perspective.

Sample Selection

Convenience sampling (Roberts – Holmes, 2011) will be used here as, being a childminder myself I have easy access to two childminding groups spanning two separate counties. All members of the groups will be given a questionnaire and have the opportunity to participate, therefore no exclusions will be made from the population.

Validity and Reliability

Golafshani (2003) describes reliability to be a consistent and true illustration of the relevant population, and validity as a question of truth and whether the data really measures the relevant research question.

Piloting the questionnaire should increase the internal validity as it will show up any flaws in its design, checking that the questions address the research question. Cohen *et al* (2011:183) describe internal validity as "the findings... must describe accurately the phenomena being researched."

External validity will be low as, nationally it is a very small sample and results will not represent or be used to generalize within the larger population .However, by asking the maximum number of childminders available, more replies give a larger amount of data, showing a wider range of opinion within the population, increasing the reliability. This is also the case by including the whole population as broader representations of opinions are accessed.

A stamped addressed envelope will be attached to the questionnaire to increase the amount of replies received as it gives an alternative method of return, and therefore will increase the validity. The completed questionnaires will be collected in a box to ensure confidentiality, which should reassure participants that they may give their honest opinions as research seeks the truth.

A lack of triangulation, using two or more data collection methods to confirm findings (Silverman, 2005) by means of a focus group will lower the validity of this research and therefore more attention must be paid to the design of the questionnaire to ensure the research question is addressed.

Validation of the type of questionnaire will also be sought from peers and the course tutor.

Considering the issue of consistency, each childminder will be asked to take the questionnaire home to fill in to avoid group opinion as group dynamics often have leaders and followers.

Ethical Considerations

Ethical Guidelines For Education Research (2011) as set out by the British Educational Research Association (BERA, 2011) will be adhered to closely to ensure the integrity of this research project.

Voluntary informed consent will be sought, in writing, by explaining to the participants the purpose and the process of the project. It will give the option to ask questions of the researcher and the freedom to withdraw at any point, ceasing participation. Informed consent is "the procedures in which individuals choose whether to participate in an investigation after being informed of facts that would be likely to influence their decisions" (Diener and Crandall, 1978 cited in Cohen *et al*, 2000:51)

Forms will be filled in anonymously to ensure confidentiality within BERA's ethical consideration of protecting the participant.

The Data Protection Act 1998 will also be closely followed. The Act demands that anyone holding records must allow access to the participant, state the purpose for data storage, and ensure secure storage of records. The Act also states that permission must be gained from the participant to share information with others and that it is their duty to ensure those third parties are allowed access, and that records will only be kept as long as necessary. Therefore data will be disposed of after the project is complete (TSO, 1998).

Regarding the cost/benefits ratio (Cohen *et al*, 2000), it is not anticipated that the research will upset people or outweigh the research worth as it is to be confidential and not of a particularly sensitive nature.

Reference List

BELL, J (2010) *Doing Your Research Project A Guide For First-Time Researchers In Education, Health And Social Science.* 5th Edition, Maidenhead, Open University Press

BRITISH EDUCATIONAL RESEARCH ASSOCIATION (2011) *Ethical Guidelines For Educational Research,* London, BERA Publications

COHEN, L, MANION, L and MORRISON, K (2000) *Research Methods In Education.* 5th Edition, London, Routledge Falmer

COHEN, L, MANION, L and MORRISON, K (2007) *Research Methods In Education.* 6th Edition, Abingdon, Routledge

COHEN, L, MANION, L and MORRISON, K (2011) *Research Methods In Education.* 7th Edition, Abingdon, Routledge

CRESWELL, J (2013) *Educational Research: Planning, Conducting And Evaluating Quantitative And Qualitative Research.* 4th Edition, Harlow, Pearson Education Ltd

DEPARTMENT FOR EDUCATION, (2012) *Statutory Framework for the Early Years Foundation Stage,* London, The National Archives

GILL, T (2007) *No Fear Growing Up In A Risk Averse Society,* London, Calouste Gulbenkian Foundation

GILLHAM, B (2007) *Developing a Questionnaire.* 2nd Edition, London, Continuum International Publishing Group

GLADWIN, M, and COLLINS, J, (2008) Anxieties And Risks, *In* Collins, J and Foley, P (Eds) *Promoting Children's Wellbeing Policy And Practice,* Bristol, The Policy Press

GOLAFSHANI, N (2003) Understanding Reliability And Validity In Qualitative Research, *The Qualitative Report* Vol.8, No.4, p597-607

HEALTH AND SAFETY EXECUTIVE (2012) *Frequently Asked Questions – Education* [online]. Available from: http://www.hse.gov.uk/services/education/faqs.htm [accessed 12/10/13]

HOWARD, J, BELLIN, W, and REES, V, (2002) *Eliciting Children's Perceptions Of Play And Exploiting Playfulness To Maximise Learning In The Early Years Classroom* [online]. Available from: http://www.leeds.ac.uk/educol/documents/00002574.htm *[accessed 05/10/13]*

JAMES, M (2012) Growing Confidence In Educational Research: Threats And Opportunities. *British Educational Research Journal* Vol.38, No. 2, p181-201

MALTHOUSE, R and ROFFEY-BARENTSEN, J, (2013) *Research Projects And Dissertations: A Collection Volume 1, London,* Thalassa Publishing Ltd

MILLER, P H (2002) *Theories of Developmental Psychology.* 4th Edition, New York, Worth Publishers

ROBERTS-HOLMES, G (2011) *Doing Your Early Years Research Project A Step-By-Step Guide.* 2nd Edition, London, SAGE Publications Ltd

SHARP, J, (2009) *Success With Your Education Research Project,* Exeter, Learning Matters Ltd

SILVERMAN, D (2005) *Doing Qualitative Research.* 2nd Edition, London, SAGE Publications Ltd

SMITH, K, TODD, M and WALDMAN, J (2009) *Doing Your Undergraduate Social Science Dissertation,* Abingdon, Routledge

THE STATIONERY OFFICE (1998) *Data Protection Act*, [online] Norwich, The

Stationery Office Ltd. Available from

http://www.legislation.gov.uk/ukpga/1998/29/contents [accessed on 01/11/13]

THE STATIONERY OFFICE (2004) *The Children Act 2004, [online] Norwich,*The

Stationery Office Ltd. Available from

http://www.legislation.gov.uk/ukpga/2004/31/section/11/enacted [accessed on

15/10/13]

WALLIMAN, N and BUCKLER, S (2008) *Your Dissertation In Education,* London, SAGE

Publications Ltd

28598212R00063

Printed in Great Britain
by Amazon